On these I ponder
Where'er I wander,
And thus grow fonder,

19 Ripley Gdns
S.W. 14

SWEET CORK OF THEE

WITH ENGRAVINGS BY THE AUTHOR

SWEET CORK
OF THEE

BY

ROBERT GIBBINGS

with engravings by the author

THE MERCIER PRESS

The Mercier Press, 4 Bridge Street, Cork
24 Lower Abbey Street, Dublin 1

©The Estate of Robert Gibbings

First published in 1951, this edition 1991

ISBN 0 85342 975 8

To
JOHN and ANNA

Printed in Ireland by Colour Books Ltd.

FOREWORD

THIS book is in a sense a continuation of *Lovely is the Lee*. I begin where I left off, with only a gap of five years. And what is five years in Ireland? A few of the young people had grown taller and a few of the old people had grown a little bent, but for the most part, from that last night when I sat in Batty Kit's cottage in 1944 until the evening when I sat in it again in the spring of 1949, it might have been no more than a night's sleep with a few heavy dreams. Only one change that I could notice. At the head of the valley, remote, among the mountains, there is a house that is no longer occupied. About a year after I left Gougane, the divil came down the chimney of that house one night. He came out through the bars of the grate and he had chains on his legs and he flew across the room and out at the window. The family were all sitting round the fire at the time, and it nearly frightened the wits out of them. They left the house next morning, and no one has lived in it since. That is the only change.

CHAPTER ONE

IN THE SPRING OF 1949 the following letter came to me in London from Gougane Barra in County Cork:

> MY DEAREST FRIEND ROBERT,
>
> How are you with the years, I hope well. I can't express in words how delighted I was to get your letter. I've been in bed sick but it put new life in me. Please God I'll see you soon. . . . Good-bye now and may God and His Blessed Mother protect you and yours.
>
> Your friend
BATTY.

What answer was there to that but to go over?

Connie Cronin was on the quay at Cork to meet me. I could see him from the ship, head and shoulders above the crowd. His car was there too, so, with scarcely a pause or delay, we raced the whole length of the Lee from tidal waters to its source. Forty-six miles of road and on it all not a dozen other cars. Here and there a ruined castle, each with its legend; here and there a lovely bridge, each with its story;

an occasional weir. All along its course, whitethorn bursting into green and blackthorn shining white and sticky buds of chestnut golden in the sunlight. Red earth combed by the harrow and young meadows striped by the roller. Pied wagtails flighting before us, and wrens like winter leaves fluttering in the hedges.

The road winds with the river, at one moment level beside untroubled waters, in a wide valley where lapwings wheel; at the next, tortuous above a torrent where salmon leap. Then for a while calmly, tracing the contours of lake shores with range beyond range of hills to south and west, the cones of Sheehy and Doughil high above them all. Finally, a game of hide-and-seek among the crags and heather-covered ridges, the road a track, the Lee a tarn, and the smell of turf fires sweet in the air. Ochre and lavender of heath and rocks and gold of bursting gorse, silver of lichens in the ink-green ling, and coral red of myrtle buds. One last mile of twists and turns, sharp hills and sudden dips, and then Gougane. In old times one needed to wash in Jordan to be cleansed, one needed to dip in Siloam for sight to be restored; but to-day, merely to stand beside the lake at Gougane Barra brings to one's whole being a peace beyond the telling.

The first man that I met as I stepped out of the car was Shaun the Post. 'You're strong as ever?' he asked. 'Wisha, my God, isn't the circumference on you grand entirely. Faith, 'twould take the big push of wind to knock you down.'

Connie's wife, Joan, and his mother, Grannie Cronin, were at the door to greet me, and while we were talking three wild swans glided through the pass and lighted on the dark water of the lake. In contrast, a black cormorant rose out of the water with its belly full of trout, and soared away over the purple rocks to the north. When I went into the

kitchen, there were Mary and Nell and Eileen. Mary, strong as ever, was before the range, shifting heavy cauldrons and kettles as if they were pint pots; Nell, quiet as ever, was getting ready a tray of tea—there's always tea going in that house; and Eileen, shy as ever, was flitting from door to door. A new-born lamb was bleating from a box in the corner. Its mother had died. Little Margaret would look after it. 'She can do anything with animals. You'd rarely see her without a string of dogs or kittens after her.'

Batty Kit came in with a bottle of whiskey under his arm. No, he wouldn't touch a drop of it: I was to put it in my room for a quiet nip. So we had a couple from another bottle, just to celebrate. He told me that the health in him was grand but the bones in him was getting stiff. The divil himself was in them.

B

5

'There 's many a man of less than eighty-two years of age is stiff in the bones,' I said. He thought maybe I was right.

'I 've got three blackthorns cut for you,' he said, 'and they 're drying inside by the chimney.'

'He 's used up his ration of butter on them,' said Connie.

'Sure, isn't it the best thing in the world to put a bit of a polish on a stick,' said Batty.

Jer Riordan came in from the mountain. ''Twas a great winter in sheep,' he said. 'No frost. But 'twas hard these past weeks. If the wind would go round to the west or the south-west, with the mist now and again and a few days' rain, there 'd soon be a fine growth of grass.'

And then the door opened and Seamus Henchy appeared. When I had last seen him, in 1944, his clothes were loose on him and he had looked almost haggard; but now he was robust, twice the man. Since our last meeting, he said, he 'd never wanted for a shilling. Did I remember him telling me then how he 'd sold the goats? I did indeed. He hadn't had as much as the price of a match that morning when he went east to help Jerry the Bridge with a bit of blasting in the little field. The war was on at the time and they weren't supposed to have any dynamite, so when they saw a strange gentleman coming towards them on the road they were sure 'twas a detective was after them. 'Jerry was changing every colour when he came on us, and what were the man's first words to him but "Have you any goats for sale?" "I have not," said Jerry. "What would you give?" I said to him. "I 'd give a pound for a good one," says he. "Then I have seven good ones," I said. With that the two of us went west to the house, and when he seen the goats he put seven pound notes into my hand.'

'So the luck has held?' I asked.

'I haven't looked back since,' said Seamus.

6

Once again the door opened, and this time it was Denny from next door who arrived. His solemn face was as poor a disguise as ever for the divilment in his eyes.

'Come on over to-night,' he said. 'There'll be a bit of a dance inside.'

'Draw up now and take your dinner,' said Joan.

So that evening I went across the yard and into Denny's kitchen. In the open hearth a turf fire was blazing enough to  light the room. Denny was sitting beside it turning the handle of the blower. 'Better than any bellows,' he said. 'If 'tis well put in 'twill redden an iron for you—I mean a horse-shoe or the like of that.' Sam, the old sheep-dog, going a bit grey about the muzzle—'no better guide on the mountains'—was there too. The room had been cleared of all furniture except the settle, a few chairs, and the cupboard that held everything from loaves of bread to turkey eggs, socks, and cartridges. A gun and its cleaning rod were suspended from the ceiling. There were about thirty people gathered there, mostly young but with a scattering of older ones and a few small children.

Old Patsy Corcoran was on the settle in the corner with a grandchild on his knee. His hat was on the back of his head, and a grey tuft of hair hung over his forehead. His face, the deep red of sorrel, had become more wrinkled, but his eyes shone as blue as ever in their frame of pale lashes.

7

'The health is not very well with me,' he said. 'But that's the way the world goes—the young ones be rising and the old ones be falling.' After a moment's pause he added, 'And hither and over, east or west, north or south, each one must hammer out his own road.'

Jimmy Duggan, eighteen stone at least, came across the room to greet me. 'So you're married since?' I asked.

'True enough,' he answered. 'She has me on the bridle-path now.'

Una, his wife, bright eyed, dark haired, dwarfed by her husband, joined us.

''Tis the tight rein he needs,' she said.

'She has me spancelled,' said Jimmy.

''Twas the grandest wedding I was ever at,' said Dan Doolan who was close by. 'There wasn't a man left standing in the latter end. They were thrown in every corner. Sure, he knocked 'em all with the white stuff.'

'What would a cat's kitten do but kill mice?' said Una.

'Jimmy is as good a man with a still as his father,' explained Mick.

'There was a fellow died, east in Ballingeary,' said Denny, 'and he went to Limbo, and he hadn't been there any time at all when he found a little bit of a stream and didn't he start making poteen. Sure they had to close the whole place down ever after.'

Conversation continued while we waited for the fiddler. I inquired about the fishing. 'If you had St. Peter in the boat with you you wouldn't catch trout this weather. 'Tis too cold,' said Mick.

'Isn't it an old saying that March doesn't go out till the twelfth of April,' said Una.

'Where's the fiddler? Where's the fiddler?' was now the talk. 'Isn't he the linchpin of the evening?' Would he be outside in the bar, they wondered.   One or two were getting anxious.

'Yerra, stay quiet,' said someone.   'He isn't wet enough yet.'

But just then the fiddler appeared.   He had been having a few pints to soften up his fingers.

Hardly had he put the bow to the strings than a dozen boys and girls were whirling round the room in a reel-set, and by the time that was finished Paddy Quill had arrived with his fiddle and another man with an accordion, and soon after that Jim Callaghan came in with his fiddle, and then four men danced a jig step, each one in turn picking up the beat on the last step of the man before him, in a fugue-like sequence of ever-increasing tempo.   After that they drew two crossed lines on the floor with chalk and four men danced 'The Peeler and the Goat,' at one moment confining their jig steps to their own particular segment and at the next leaping from one division to another while all the time keeping to the jig time.   And when they 'd danced a reel-step and a hornpipe, someone called for a song, and Batty Kit's son, Batt the Bus—he 's a bus driver by profession—sang *Noreen Bawn*, and then Paddy Quill sang *Mount Massy, the Pride of Macroom*.   Square dances and more jigs followed, and than Shaun Pat gave us *The Buck from Bunane*, a ballad commemorating an almost recent event:

'Young lads and fair lassies, I claim your attention,
    And then will I tell you what happened to those
    Who left Ballingeary on the 15th of August
    And went back to Borlin in search of a goat.'

Many verses describe the climb over the hills to Bunane, the capture of the wild goat in the Borlin mountains, and the return of the hunters with their booty.   Unfortunately,

while celebrating their success, the temptation to set free the
goat overcame a young lad of the district.

'So when they came out after drinking some porter,
In this hotel of Cronin's in lovely Gougane,
They went to the place where they 'd left the bold hero
And found he was half the way back to Bunane.

Then they began shouting and loudly lamenting,
The company all then began for to cry;
For they must look out for another bold hero
Or the goats of the country would surely run dry.'

''Twas myself cut the rope,' whispered old Patsy to me.
'Myself and none other. I didn't tell them for twenty years.
They 'd have destroyed me.'

The company now thought it was my turn and, not for-
getting my little adventure with a still of which I told in
Lovely is the Lee, called on me for *Red is the Rose*. But this
time, wet or dry, I couldn't even get into the vall-ey, let
alone get out of it after. So they all joined in and helped me,
and we finished together in a grand conclusion. After that
there was more dancing. From what I could see of the clock
when I rose to go it was twenty past two, but next morning
they told me that it was ten past four when I left the house,
which might be a lesson to any man how time flies.

CHAPTER TWO

SOON AFTER I REACHED Gougane, an old friend of mine, Tim Leahy, a farmer, told me that he had to go to Killarney. His wife's uncle had recently died in America leaving her some money. She came from Killarney and the money had been left to her through a solicitor in the town. She was none too strong and couldn't travel, so he was going to see the lawyer for her. Would I like to come with him for the drive?

So we started off in his car, east through Ballingeary and then north up a steep valley with rugged hills on either side and the Bunsheelin River tumbling through its boulder-strewn course towards us. From there across the saddle of the mountain, with the Paps of Dana, far to the north, dominating a nearer range of hills. These twin mountains take their name from Dana, mother of the Irish gods, who in pagan times was worshipped in Munster as the goddess of plenty. According to bardic chroniclers, the *Tuatha Dea*

11

Danaan, the People of the Goddess Dana, on being conquered by the Milesians centuries before the Christian era, held council among themselves and decided henceforth to live underground in the hills.   There they built palaces for themselves, resplendent with gold and precious stones, and there according to some people they still live, being known to-day as *shee* or fairies.

Now the road curled round the heads of valleys, great loops of it lassooing outcrops of rock.   It had become scarcely

more than a track, narrow, uneven in surface, rich in steep gradients, poorly supplied with any protection on the sides of precipices, and for variety well endowed with hairpin bends.   It was on one of its most spectacular twists that we met a dozen piebald ponies, straggling unattended and grazing on the verges of the road.   They were the advance party of a band of tinkers who we came upon at the next critical manœuvre.

It transpired that these tinkers were of the O'Brien tribe and, as we talked, an old man mentioned having served in the 1914–18 war.

'In the Munsters, I suppose,' I said.

'In the *Royal* Munster Fusiliers,' he replied. 'The stateliest band of men that ever marched a road. Sure, when Queen Victoria came to Killarney 'twas the Munsters had to march down the road ahead of her. She said she wouldn't be safe with any other regiment. Tell me,' he added, 'did you know Colonel Macgillicuddy?'

'I did,' I said.

'Oh then, he was the grand man. Do you know what he did one day on the barrack square at Tralee? Faith, he paraded every man of the regiment before him, and his lady was alongside of him, and what did she do but hand out a pint of stout to each and every one of us. Six hundred and fifty pints she handed out.'

I said I was sorry there wasn't a pub near by where I could hand him a couple of pints. He said the nearest one would be 'Hannah's' and that was three miles west on the road. I told him to call in on his way back and he 'd find a drop waiting for him.

Wouldn't I like to buy a couple of nice piebalds? he asked as we parted.

Hannah claims that her pub is the highest in Ireland. It is certainly on high ground, about a thousand feet above sea level, with the Cork and Kerry boundary running almost through her kitchen. Over its door is the inscription: 'Seven Days. Hannah McCarthy licensed to sell spirets to be consumbed in premises.' As hotels go it is a small one, not more than a room and a half on the ground floor with probably the same accommodation upstairs. In the smaller room below is a bar, in the larger one an open fireplace with an iron crane from which hang the usual pots for spuds or mash for the animals. There are chairs and a wooden settle for visitors.

'You 're high up in the world,' I said to Hannah as I went in.

''Tis only a small little step from here to heaven,' she said.

''Tis cold to-day,' I said.

''Tis colder in the winter,' she replied.

Jer Lucey, from near Kilgarvan, had been sitting in the corner, unnoticed. 'You wouldn't be a bit surprised to see the snow twenty feet thick up here of a day in January,' he said. 'You see, you 're nearer to the sky and you 'd get more of it than they would in the valley. Wasn't that a fierce pile of rain we had last week?' he added.

'It looks better now,' I suggested.

'It 'll be better surely,' said Hannah. 'The floor is sweating and the soot has been coming down the chimney, and the two of them together is always a sign of good weather.'

'We wouldn't fall out with a bit of it now,' said Jer.

'Hannah,' said Tim, pointing at me, 'could you do anything for this man?'

'What way would I do it?' asked Hannah.

'The usual way,' said Tim. In an undertone he added: 'He 's mad to be married.'

'And why isn't he fixed already?'

'He 's shy,' said Tim.

'Isn't it queer to be like that, and he with the years on him.'

'He 's innocent, too,' said Tim.

'Faith, then, a man could live and die up here as innocent as the day he was born. Tell me,' she said, 'in what sort of a way would he be?'

'Oh then, in a damn fine sort of a way,' said Tim.

'Then he wouldn't be wanting the house east on the hill?' she said.

'What rent is it?' I asked.

'A shilling a year, paid quarterly,' she replied.

'He has a fine house of his own,' said Tim, 'and all he wants is a wife.'

'She 'd have to be strong,' said Jer.

'He 's heavy all right,' said Tim.

'I know a girl would quieten him,' said Hannah.

'Did you hear about Seamus Cooney that married last spring?' said Jer to me.

'I know of him,' I said. 'He bred greyhounds.'

'He did that, and he hunted them, too. He was mad to be after a hare. But she made him give it all up. 'Twas about a month after he got married that he was out by himself in the bogs, without ever a hound, and a big jack hare jumps up under his feet and starts lepping about in front of him. "Faith," says Seamus to the hare, "if you 'd been married a month you wouldn't be lepping about like that."'

'Come on, Tim,' I said. 'I 'd feel safer in Killarney.'

'You see how shy he is,' said Tim, as we went out of the door.

'I think the two pair of ye is airy men but ye 're the divil's own rascals,' said Hannah.

We hadn't gone two miles on the road to Kilgarvan before we stopped to give a lift to a woman carrying a heavy basket.

'You 're a fine young girl to be walking the roads,' said Tim.

'Isn't it time someone told me that now, and me forty?' she said. 'And what 's more, aren't you a fine block of a man to be driving a car.'

'Don't believe a word he says,' I told her. 'He 's got me into trouble to-day already.'

'Is it jealous you are?' she said.

'He 's fixed,' said Tim. 'Hannah has the right woman for him, and they 're only waiting for harvest.'

'Begor, I think harvest twelve months will be early,' said our companion.

It was market day when we arrived in Killarney and the town was full of horse and donkey carts piled high with hay or seedling cabbages. We were early for Tim's appointment. That didn't matter; he had a bit of shopping to do for the wife, he said.

He manœuvred the car through the crowded narrow streets and pulled up outside a small china shop. No sooner inside than he introduced me to Miss Nagle, the proprietress, as Colonel Nagle, a relative of hers from England who had come to look up his Irish relations.

Miss Nagle, a tall, gaunt woman in a stiff black dress, peered at me through a pair of dark spectacles, one glass of which was badly splintered.

'Big estates he has,' said Tim. 'Some of the biggest in England.'

'And what part of England would they be in?'

'Devonshire,' said Tim.

'I didn't know there were any of the family in Devonshire,' said Miss Nagle to me.

'I didn't know myself till a short while ago,' I said. ''Twas only recently I came in for the property.'

'Would you like to buy a cup?' she asked. 'Here's a nice one now, with "A Present from Killarney" written on it. Aren't they having great trouble with the Government in England?'

''Tis a teapot he's after,' said Tim.

'Well then, I have only one of the big brown ones. I dunno will the Germans ever settle down, and what will the Russians do next? 'Twould be too large for him, I suppose,' she said, taking a teapot from the shelf and handing it to me.

'Yerra, not at all,' said Tim. 'Sure, his house is as big as a mansion. Isn't that just the thing for you now, colonel? It is to be sure! I 'll pay for it,' he added. 'The colonel forgets his money.'

That purchase completed, we walked a dozen yards down the street and into an ironmonger's.

'Mr. MacCarthy,' said Tim to the man behind the counter. 'This is Admiral MacCarthy from the British Navy. Maybe he 's a relation of yours.'

'He 's a namesake, anyway,' said Mr. MacCarthy.

'He 's after coming out of the war, and 'twas him destroyed most of the Germans.'

'Well now,' said Mr. MacCarthy, looking me up and down. I could see that one or two others had appeared from other parts of the shop and were looking me up and down also.

'His ship was like a colander before he 'd finished.'

'Glory be to God!'

'And that 's what we 've come in after now,' continued Tim.

'Not a battleship, I hope,' said Mr. MacCarthy.

'No, but a colander,' said Tim. 'The admiral collects them. Every town he goes into he buys one. He says they remind him of the way his ships was after the battle.'

'Well, here 's a nice one now, sir,' said Mr. MacCarthy, lifting one off a hook and handing it to me.

'Let me have a look at it for you,' said Tim, taking it out of my hand. He examined it carefully. 'It 's just what you want,' he said.

Something made me rub my eyes as he spoke.

'You see,' he whispered to Mr. MacCarthy, 'he gets very emotional. He 's forgetful, too. I have to pay everything for him.'

Tim handed the money across the counter and we left. Now it was time for his appointment so, leaving me at a street corner, he promised to pick me up at the same place in an hour's time.

Left to myself I wandered back towards the market-place. Business for the day was nearly over, but men were still transferring hay from lorries on to carts. It had come in from the big farms and been sold to farmers who had but small holdings. A few laden donkey carts still remained in the yard, while the owners were 'wetting their deals' in the houses across the street. A young bull was tethered to a cart wheel.

I was making a few quick drawings of faces and figures when a man coming up behind me bid me good day. 'Good day to you, good day, good day,' he said.

Not having noticed him coming I jumped at his first words.

'Begor, I knocked a start out of you,' he said. 'I did, I did, I did.' His jovial red face shone through thick black stubble, the narrow brim of his old felt hat drooped all round his head.

'I was drawing,' I said, 'and I didn't see you coming.'

'Begor, you're right,' he said. 'You're right, you're right. You didn't see me, of course, you didn't, you didn't.' He looked at my rough sketch of an old man. 'God Almighty, but you've got him, you've got him. That's old Mick, with his broken nose and all—a great fighter ever. He's a cousin of mine—he is, he is, he is. Oh, indeed, he is.
He went to America in '99, in the year '99, and he come back six years after for a holiday—six years after. Three

pounds he paid to come back—three pounds for an excursion, and he 's here since. He is, oh faith, he is, he is.'

'You couldn't get back from America for three pounds now,' I said.

'Begor, you 're right, you 're right—you couldn't, you couldn't.'

'Will you come on, Pat?' called a woman's voice from beyond the railings.

'I will, I will, I will,' he answered. 'Good-bye now and good luck to you—good luck, good luck, good luck,' he said to me, and I found myself calling after him: 'Good-bye, good-bye, good-bye!' Oh, indeed I did, I did.

Tim was waiting for me at the corner. His visit had taken him a shorter time than he had expected. Everything was in order, he said. They 'd be getting between three and four hundred pounds in no time at all. He had had a couple of drinks and was 'in good oil.'

'We 'll go home by Kenmare,' he said. ''Tis a small piece longer, but there 's a cousin of mine there would like to hear the news.'

From the town we took the Muckross road, with its high walls shutting out all view of the lakes for miles.

'The richer the land the higher the walls,' said Tim.

'There are no high walls at Gougane,' I said.

'There 's no rich land,' he answered.

'Only rich hearts,' I suggested. Tim smiled.

'There 's richness in the air,' he said. 'When I come back from a day in the mountains after the sheep I feel cleansed. 'Tis as if I 'd been walking in heaven.'

At last we were clear of the stone barricades and could catch glimpses of the lakes and mountains through a screen of oak- and holly- and birch-trees. Here is a forest unspoiled by man, its floor a wild confusion of moss and fern-encrusted rocks and tangled roots of trees. 'You should see it in June,' said Tim, 'with the rhododendrons pouring like a purple flood through the trees.' Three wild deer trotted across the road ahead of us and three more, a little further away, stood for a while in the centre of the road until we were close upon them. I told him how the red deer imported into New Zealand from Scotland had already accommodated themselves so well to the southern hemisphere that their rutting season had changed from the usual September and October at home to March and April, which are the autumn months in New Zealand. I mentioned, too, that the same deer had multiplied to such an extent in their new home that they had become almost as great plagues as the mongoose in Jamaica or the rabbits in Australia.

He said that someone had imported ground food for the trout into a lake near Gougane, with the result that all the big fish now grazed about on the bottom and wouldn't look at a fly.

By this time we had climbed to the Ladies' View. Below us, island-dotted lakes spread themselves among the purple hills, whose lower slopes were richly quilted with green. Killarney is one of the few places in the world that is better than what is said of it. Nobody could be disappointed in what it has to give, nobody could but be flabbergasted by what it shows. In any other country it would be exploited to an unbearable degree; as it is, there is little to detract from the natural scene. If a stage Irishman does occasionally put in an appearance, his performance is a good one. It is easier for him to earn a living by the lakeside than on the boards of a music-hall. One of them, a bugler, has been at the same job for forty years. He meets you among some of the most precipitous cliffs and 'blows the echo' for you. The chords repeat from side to side of the valley, and you hear the same notes many times. Then he puts his hands to his mouth and shouts: 'Here's a fine hearty man!' Again and again this flattering description comes back to you from the hills. Then he calls: 'A fine generous gentleman!' Again and again you hear '. . . generous gentleman.' The next move is left to you.

The main tourist trip, that through the Gap of Dunloe, is one that I have made several times during the past forty years, each time fearing disillusionment, each time being more than recompensed. On my last visit I dropped in to 'Kate Kearney's Cottage,' a rendezvous famed in song, a house frequented by all visitors. At one side of the room was a small table of souvenirs for sale, at the other side a small bar. While patronizing the latter, I mentioned to the proprietor that it was fifteen years since I had been in the house, and in the discussion that followed I forgot to pay for my refreshment. It was only when I was leaving that I remembered. 'Why didn't you remind me?' I asked. 'Ah,' he said, 'you'll be passing again.'

The first time I passed that way was forty years ago, when I was carrying out one of my earliest commissions as an artist. It was given to me on the Southern Railway in England, by an elderly colonel from Aberdeen, because at Haslemere we had found ourselves on the wrong side of the station as our train was leaving. 'Jump!' I said to his wife, taking a grip on her arm as the whistle blew. We ran across the rails and I pushed her into a carriage. The colonel, breathless, followed us and clambered in as the train gathered speed. We then introduced ourselves. 'It's only an Irishman would do that,' he said. Before we reached London, he said to me: 'The happiest holiday I've ever had was by the Gap of Dunloe. Go down and paint me a picture there.'

The only difference between the Gap then and now is that

in those days there was no law and order among the pony
boys in the pursuit of their clients.   When the brakes and
side-cars arrived, full of tourists from Killarney town, there
would be a general scramble and jostle, each boy pulling and
dragging whoever he could get hold of, hoisting and pushing
till they were in the saddle.   In those days women wore long
skirts.   'Arrah, never mind your legs, lady, the pony can't
look back at all.'

To-day there is a pony-master, and each animal and its
owner must await their turn.   There is also a mounting stone.

The second time that I rode through the Gap was with A. E.
Coppard when we were collaborating in the creation of
'RUMMY, that noble game, expounded in prose, poetry,
diagram, and engravings by A. E. Coppard and Robert
Gibbings with an account of certain diversions into the
mountain fastnesses of Cork and Kerry: printed and published
at The Golden Cockerel Press, Waltham Saint Lawrence,
Berkshire, 1932.'   He was writing the text and I was to
perpetrate the pictures.   Let his words tell the tale:

'Killarney is a grand spot. . . .   We went in a jaunting-car
from the town, on a long winding road towards the huge hill
of Carrantuohill, until we came to a break in the Reeks, the
Tomies, and the Purple Mountain, which our jarvey declared
"forms the formation of the celebrated Gap of Dunloe."
At the Gap we were cajoled by a horde of ponies and boys
into hiring horses for crossing the pass to the lake, a journey
of miles and more.   Horseback is torture to the likes of me,
and we seemed to jog on up and up over rocks and bogs and
streams for hours and hours, my cursed boy screwing the tail
of the horse and urging it ever on until I told him I had delicate hams and was wishful of repose.   An hour of such sport
had revealed to me that I was being greatly massacred from

the heels up. The sunlight throve whenever it could, and there were a few flaws of rain. The mountains,

> "Torn from Pelorus, or the shattered side
> Of thundering Etna,"

were blue, gold, black, grey, green; were smooth, craggy, fair, foul, quiet, malignant, benign; indeed they were everything mountains could be that you had never thought of. Said I to my boy:

'"Why is this pass called the Gap of Dunloe?"'

'"Well," he said, "that is the name of it, you see."'

'. . . A man came out of a hole in the pass and blew his trumpet for us to hear the echoes. A woman came out of a shop and wanted to sell us some cups and saucers. A lady fell off her horse and wouldn't get on again. If I could have done the same I would, but I could not; though it was agony to stay on, it would have been crucifixion to move. . . . Down by the lakeside a boat was waiting with happy boatmen and food and tipple. And as they rowed they sang, and as they sang I swore I would surely do it all again.'

It was in the Gap of Dunloe that another author, when on her honeymoon, met with an accident. In a letter from Cork dated 27th July 1854, four weeks after her marriage, Charlotte Brontë wrote to Catherine Winkworth:

'. . . We have been to Killarney. I will not describe it a bit. We saw and went through the Gap of Dunloe. A sudden glimpse of a very grim phantom came on us in the Gap. The guide had warned me to alight from my horse as the path was now very broken and dangerous. I did not feel afraid, and declined. We passed the dangerous part. The horse trembled in every limb, and slipped once, but did not fall. Soon after she (it was a mare) started, and was unruly for a minute. However, I kept my seat. My husband went to her head and led her. Suddenly, without any apparent cause, she seemed to go mad—reared, plunged. I was thrown on the stones right under her. My husband did not see that I had fallen, he still held her. I saw and felt her kick, plunge, trample round me. I had my thoughts about the moment—its consequences—my husband—my father. When my plight was seen, the struggling creature was let loose. She sprang over me. I was lifted off the stones, neither bruised by the fall or touched by the mare's hoofs. Of course, the only feeling left was gratitude for more sakes than my own.'

Whether it was the face of Death that Charlotte meant by the 'very grim phantom,' or whether she referred to some apparition which scared her horse, it is hard to say. I made inquiries of many, but could hear of no tradition of a spectre, other than the serpent which inhabits one of the lakes. This creature must assuredly take first place among all the 'last serpents' of Ireland, for it is still alive, though confined in an iron chest with nine bolts on it. St. Patrick enticed it into the box with a gallon of porter and then clapped the lid down on it. He threw the chest into the lake, and it is the struggles of the reptile at the bottom that cause the waves on the surface.

To-day the 'path' is so good that a pony trap or even a small motor car can make the ascent, but I do not recommend either. Once on the pony's back you can leave everything to the animal. There isn't a stone on the road that it doesn't know. To use the reins would be an insult. Sit forward going uphill, lean back on the steep, southward slope, and you will be carried easily along the winding trail, terraced with lakes among deeply fissured bastions of rock and cataracts of boulders, and down the far side to the lake's edge

where the boat awaits you.   Thence you will be rowed the
whole course of the enchanted waters and landed close to the
town.   You will hear in rich phrases the oft-told tale of
the chieftain O'Donoghue who on a May morning may be seen
rising out of the lake in shining armour on a white steed,
followed by young men and maidens garlanded with flowers
and tripping the waters as though they were a spring meadow.
You will hear many other tales, too, credible or incredible
according to your fancy.   One thing you will not hear is
any tale that could describe the ever-changing majesty and
loveliness that pervade those lakes.

CHAPTER THREE

FROM THE LADIES' VIEW, Tim and I drove on up the hill to Windy Gap, opening up vista after vista of distant hills dappled as a panther's skin by drifting flecks of cloud. Then through a wilderness of rocks and bogs, stones with sharp edges cloven by recent frosts, boulders planed smooth by the ice of a distant age, until below us we could see the road to Kenmare winding down the valley, glistening after a shower like the track of a snail. On our right a succession of combes and crater-like basins among the brows and spurs of the hills.

'It was about a mile to the west, over across that mountain there,' said Tim, 'that a man by the name of Lynch and his wife were living. They had a thatched cottage with two compartments, and in the one was himself and his wife and in the other was a cow and a cock and seven hens. And the house was set in the cleft of a valley with the mountains steep on either side of them, and one day a snowdrift came down on top of them and they couldn't get out and they had no food. So they killed and ate a hen and made soup of its bones, and that lasted them two days, and then they killed another hen and that lasted them another two days, and then they killed another hen and that lasted them another two days. And so it went on till there was only one hen left and the cock, and the husband wanted to kill the cock but his wife wouldn't let him do this, for the crowing of a cock keeps the fairies away. And while they were arguing, there was a great commotion in the chimney and down came a grouse followed by a hawk—the chimney, you see, was the only bit of shelter the grouse could find. And so they killed the two of them and that lasted

them three days.   And after that a great darkness came over
the sky and the husband looked out.   "It 's going to rain,"
he said.   And he was right, for the rain came down and
washed away all the snow, and them and the cow and the
cock and the one hen was saved.'

Now another panorama opened before us, serrated mountain crests tipped with cloud enclosing a throng of lesser
hills.   I inquired about his cousin who we were going to
visit.

"'Twas below in that valley she used to live,' said Tim.
'She was married and had three children and they had a farm,
and one day the husband walked out on her.   Dead, buried,
and prayed for he was for twenty-five years, and not a day but
she 'd be sounding his fine qualities.   And then one night
there was a knocking at the door and she opened it and a
man came in.   "Who are you?" said she.   "Your husband," said he.   "You 're not," said she.   "I am," said
he.   "I wouldn't know you," said she.   "I wouldn't know
you," said he.   So then he sat down and he told her this and
he told her that, to kind of remind her.   "Have you got the
wart still on your neck?" she said.   "I have," he said.
"On the right side of your neck, below your shirt?" says
she.   "That 's true," he said.   "Open up your shirt,"
says she, "and let me see it."   So he opened the shirt for her
and there was the wart.   "What made you walk out on us?"

27

she said. "Drove out I was," said he. "Well then, you can walk out again in the morning," says she, "for the farm is sold and the daughters are married and the son and myself are leaving next week." "Where will you be going?" he asked. "Never mind where we 'll be going. You did well enough without us for twenty-five years, we 'll manage without you for another twenty-five." So he slept on the settle that night, and when they woke up in the morning he was gone, and they never seen him since and that was four years ago. She has a pub this side of Kenmare now.'

In due course Tim pulled up the car outside a small public-house. Over the door I read: 'Mary Helena Brennan, licensed to sell tobacco and spirits.' Tim led the way in.

Two men were sitting on a bench: one, almost a dwarf, short and thickset, with black hair showing under his mustard-coloured cap; the other tall and lean, grey and elderly, leaning forward on his stick. He wore a high felt hat that had once been green. His light homespun jacket and trousers were faded almost to sheep colour. A big patch on each knee was stitched with blue wool. I soon discovered that though his eyes were open they were sightless. Whereas the little man's features were broad and squat, the other's were finely cut with high forehead and long, lean nose. A third, a fisherman in blue gansey and trousers and a cap back to front on his head, was leaning against the counter. As we said 'good day' to each other, Mary Helena came in from the back.

'Wisha, welcome, Tim! How 's the health? Good, I hope? Welcome to you, too,' she said to me after I had been introduced. 'Faith, you 're an elegant lump of a man, wherever you come from. And what 's the news? Nothing strange and nothing new, I suppose?'

'I have a word for you later on,' said Tim. 'Give us a drink first.'

Mary Helena was a big buxom woman of about fifty years of age, though her sleek black hair and dark sparkling eyes suggested that she might have been ten years younger. The skin on her neck and arms was clear and smooth as a child's.

'You 've had your bite?' she asked.

'Not one thrawneen,' said Tim.

'We shall rectify that,' she said, handing us drinks. 'Wouldn't the two of ye sit down?'

'Jerry,' said Tim to the blind man, 'did you ever meet a writer?'

'I did, faith, when I was a young man and had the sight, I 'd go and visit every writer and poet in Munster, and when the eyes grew dark in me, didn't they all come and visit me.'

'I 've brought a writer with me to-night,' said Tim. 'A great one, I tell you.'

'Don't believe a word of it,' I said. ''Tis only an occasional story that I write.'

'I could tell you stories from the beginning of the world to the end of the world,' said Jerry. 'I could tell you of every chieftain in Ireland. I could tell you how eighty horses with two men on each went north from Kerry to fight King Billy at the Battle of the Boyne, and you couldn't count the number they killed. And I could tell you about a rock like an eagle that 's on top of one of the mountains in Kerry, and below it in the side of the cliff is a cave with a yellow door, and whenever a chief of the O'Sullivans is going to die the door will break open and a keen will come out of it like a great blast in a storm, and then it will shut again.' He spoke in a deep rolling cadence as if he were declaiming poetry. 'And I could tell you,' he went on, 'of the rising in '67, the White Boys they called it. I was only a scrapeen of a boy at the time, but I remember it as well as I know the glass in my hand. I remember a neighbour of mine, a grand foxy young boy by the name of Stevens. He had on him a woman's uniform and rigging and all, and sewn up inside the shift was a message. And he was hid between twelve firkins turned upside down in the back of a common cart. Sitting up in a sop of hay he was, and there was no notice taken of him. He went safe through all.'

'That was a smart trick sure enough,' said the dwarf.

'You remember about the cat and the fox?' said Jerry. 'They met in a wood, and it was a very sunny day, and they were sunning themselves and having a grand time. But in the height of their glory they heard the sound of the hounds. "What will we do?" "Oh," says the cat, "I suppose you will be able to manage, but I have only the one trick. 'Tis you have all the tricks in the world." "I have ten tricks,' said the fox; "in case one of them fails me I will use another one." "Having such a lot of tricks you will be able to get out," said the cat, "but I have only the one and God help me." The hounds was getting nearer and nearer, and the cat and the fox was getting more distressed, and more and more. And the fox said: "By God," he said, "I think we shall have to be hooking it, we must be saying good-bye." "You will be all right," said the cat, "but I have only the one trick and that is no good to any man. A man that has ten will be able to manage anywhere in the world." With that the cat ran up the highest tree in the forest, and when he was up at the top he looked down and says he to the hounds that was passing below: "Miaow!" But they could not get up that tree. 'Twas no good for them to try. Sure, a dog can't climb a tree. So they followed the fox with the ten tricks, and didn't they catch him and tear him to pieces. So one good trick is better than ten bad ones, you see.'

'A sound ass is more use than a spavined horse,' said the dwarf.

While the story-telling was going on, Tim had followed his cousin through the door at the back. Now Jerry took his glass from under the seat and finished its contents. The dwarf tapped on the counter with the base of his own glass but got no reply. Helena's attention seemed fully occupied in the other room.

'Tell me,' continued Jerry, 'did you ever hear of Owen Ruadh, Owen the Red? He was a poet, and he had a wonderful way with the women. 'Twas said he didn't know the half of the children that he left after him, but I don't think that would be true. He was a real crafty man, too, with the money, though he'd be generous enough at times. One day he met a boy on the road, and something in the boy pleased him. "The next time I see you," said he to the boy, "I'll give you a shilling." The words were hardly out of his mouth before the boy lepped over the fence and away with him round a lump of rock that was in the field and in less than one minute and three-quarters he was back in the middle of the road a hundred yards beyond to meet Owen Ruadh. And what do you think the poet said to the boy when he gave him the shilling? "Begor, you must be a son of mine," he said.'

'How do you remember it all?' I asked.

'Memory, do you see,' said Jerry. 'If you haven't that you couldn't remember yesterday, you couldn't remember the middle of the day yesterday. But that wouldn't happen to me, blind though I be. I need not tell you at all, because you would understand it yourself, that many people are careless about any anecdote of history, but when I had the sight I would turn every page of the paper and search the whole thing column by column. I would not leave the length of my finger unread.'

The dwarf tapped on the counter again. Then, turning to me he asked: 'Did ye ever hear of the rock near to us here, with stones like rolls of butter on top of it? If you take away one of the rolls of an evening, there 'll be another there in the morning.'

'There was a stone near Kilmalkedar,' said the fisherman, 'with basins hollowed into it. And there was a cow with an enchantment on her would come in from the sea and she 'd milk herself into whatever kind of a vessel would be put under her. And if there was no one there with a vessel she 'd go to the stone and stand overight it and milk herself into the basins. She was a wonderful help to the poor people. But there was a woman with blackness in her heart agin her neighbours, and one day she put a sieve under the udder instead of a pail. When the cow took a look behind to see how the pail was getting on and she seen the white stream of her milk spread on the ground, she let out of her mouth one big gust of a sigh—'twas like the blast of a smith's bellows—and with that she dropped down dead.'

As he finished the story Helena opened the door and called me into the kitchen. 'Come on now, Mister, and have a sup of tea.' She went behind the bar and served a round of drinks. 'Bring yours with you now,' she said to me. The sup of tea was three fried eggs, three rashers, and as many sausages.

Helena was in high spirits. What she 'd be getting would pay off the last little bit due on the house. 'As I may go before my God,' she said, 'it 's the best news ever.' While Tim and I sat at the table she kept moving about the room, singing snatches of songs interspersed with comments.

'"Nothing else would matter in the world that day . . ."
Wasn't it damn generous of him now?

"We can go on living in the same old way . . ."
Wisha, God be praised for all.'

On our way home, I said to Tim: 'Whatever made the husband walk out on a fine woman like that?'

'There 's only one person knows that,' he said, 'and that 's himself. Isn't it an old saying, "'Tis only the man that wears the shoe knows where it pinches.'''

CHAPTER FOUR

IT WAS A SOFT DAY, 'warm but cool through all.'
Elly Leary, wife of Timmy Batt Kit, and Kate Hyde, wife
of Patty Cronin, had come into Denny's kitchen to give a
day's work, cutting *skiollauns*—sometimes called seed potatoes. It was the 11th of April and the spuds should be
in as soon as ever the weather allowed it. A few had already
been planted, but in the mountains, for fear of the frosts, little
is done about early potatoes. Elly and Kate sat on a bench on
the far side of the big open fire. I was sitting in the corner of
the settle on the near side. It is my favourite seat in that
house; there 's something about its width and the slope of its
panelled back that suits my curves. An English visitor, a
retired major, was beside me. Lassie, the red setter, lay on
the cement floor in front of the fire, with her legs stretched
out on either side of a black kettle. Patsy, a piebald cat, was
sitting up straight alongside her, and a big pot of spuds was
hanging over the reddening turf.

'Patsy is a fright altogether for catching young rabbits,'
said Elly. 'He goes out in the meadow and he lies down and

34

he rolls in the grass, and the rabbits have no fear of him at all, and then he walks over a step or two nearer to them and he rolls again, and 'tis the way the rabbits think he is playing. And all of a sudden he makes a jump at one of them, and with one nip he has it killed. He takes it west then to the hay shed and he eats it.'

Between the two women on the bench was a tub of seed potatoes, between them on the floor was a smaller tub, and in front of each was an open sack. As each of them took a potato from the larger tub, she sliced it into two or more portions, according to the number of 'eyes' it had. Each piece with an eye was dropped into a sack, the remaining portions that were blind were thrown into the tub on the floor. They would be given to the cows with a little meal mixed through.

Denny dropped in from time to time to throw a remark, relevant or otherwise.

'Have you the cinders saved for the skiollauns?' asked Elly one time when he appeared.

'I threw them in the face of the storm a while back,' said Denny.

In the old times it was the regular custom to keep some ashes from the Christmas fire and to sprinkle them on the seed potatoes at the time of planting. It is still done in a few houses. It was believed, too, that if you threw a handful of the ashes into an approaching storm it would drive it back.

'The priest went out yesterday,' said Denny, 'and he hooked three salmon and he lost them all. He split his net and he broke his rod—they said cattle went be-damned altogether at Bantry Fair—and Paddy Quill mended the rod with a couple of boot laces and with the first cast, after, he landed a two-pound trout.'

Two men arrived in a lorry from Macroom with provisions for the bar. They said they 'd passed two funerals on the road.

'Did you ever hear,' asked Denny, 'that if two men are buried on the same day, the one that 's the second to be buried will have to carry water for the other fellow in Purgatory?'

'Did you ever hear about the two funerals that met at the cross at Kilmichael?' said Murty, the taller of the two lorry men. ''Twas some years back, and 'twas a great rush to see which of them would get round the corner first. And they were shouldering the coffins because there was no hearses in those days. And one way and the other in the scramble to get first on the road the two coffins met end to end and all the men started fighting. They put the two coffins down on the side of the road and they pitched into each other. And neither of them was winning until a big strap of a woman took off her shoe, and 'twas a shoe with a big heel on it, and didn't she attack the men that was against her. She hit one after the other of them between the two eyes with the heel of her shoe, and she stretched ten of them. 'Twas only when the rest of the party saw the ten stretched that they gave up. So when the woman seen that she had them all beat: "Take off the lid of the coffin," says she, "and you 'll see Jerry inside laughing."'

The major was a bit lost by all this. He turned to me.

'Have you written anything since your book about the Lee?' he asked.

'I 've written one about the South Sea islands,' I told him.

'You 've been to the Pacific?'

'I spent two years there.'

'How sensible! I always think it wise to visit a place before one writes about it.'

36

Now it was my turn to feel lost.

'May I get a few drinks?' I asked.

'Help yourself,' said Denny, who was now basting a potful of ducks that hung over the fire.

It is one of my privileges in that house that I may act as deputy barman, but when I went to put money in the till I had nothing in my pocket but a two-shilling piece. 'I'll owe you the rest,' I said.

'The mould that made that coin made many another,' said Denny.

'What's that he's saying?' asked the major.

'There was a man after committing a crime,' said Denny. 'He was a cousin of mine, and 'twas a small thing anyway, but they found a footprint and they went along to his house and took one of his shoes and it fitted the print, so they took him into court and 'twas like things were going bad with him till the judge says: "The last that made that shoe made many another shoe too." The judge was a cousin of mine, so d'you see they were kind of related. After that they let him off.'

'He means you've got plenty more of the same coin,' said Elly.

Denny got busy again with the ducks. The major had given him a cigar which he now held in one hand behind his back, while with the other he ladled the hot fat over the carcases in the pot. A rap on the counter outside recalled my attention to the bar, and I went out to answer as best I could.

There was only one man there, an elderly man, thin and grey.

'So you found your way back again?' he said. 'Ah well, you know your horse-box.'

I recognized him as one I had met on board the *Innisfallen*

D

when crossing from Fishguard. It was a wild and rough night, but for all that I couldn't help creeping up on deck next morning as we went between the heads at the entrance to Cork harbour. It seemed at first as if there was no one else on deck, but as I walked for'ard I noticed a man kneeling behind one of the double seats. I stopped, not wishing to disturb him, but he had seen me. 'I came up to have a squint at the points as we came through,' he said.

'Is it long since you 've seen them?' I asked.

'Forty years and twenty-three days,' he replied.

So now he joined us for a drink, and then because there was a gleam of sunshine he and I went out and wandered up the track behind the house. A willow-wren whispered from a holly bush, a chaffinch shouted from a larch. We could see a pair of herons nest-building in the trees on the island. The grass on either side of the lane was close nibbled by the sheep, the soil indented by their feet. The ground was soft after the rain. Moist mosses shone gold and green, and sunlit hills, radiant with gorse, contrasted with shaded nooks glowing with violets. At the head of the lake the clumps of young larches shone like emeralds among the purple hills.

'Many the time I 've wanted the white cream of the lime-stone to be spattered on my boots,' said my companion. 'Many the time I 've wanted the black cushions of the turf to be springing under my feet.'

In a small field beside the lane, five men were preparing the land for the skiollauns. A pair of grey horses were pulling the plough, one of them 'a great lazy hulking divil, throwing his feet in all directions,' the other a lighter animal pulling all its weight. The green sod was curling over from the blade of the plough like the curving of a wave as it runs across a sloping shore. There are rocks in the ground and it needs one man to drive the horses while another guides the steel. Three men were filling every third furrow with manure, the gathering of soiled furze litter from the cow-sheds and stables. In this the spuds would be planted, and at the first earthing the furrow on either side would be turned back on them. The manure had already been carted and stood in heaps about the field, the placing of the heaps care-fully calculated to save much carrying on the forks. The men with the forks could just keep ahead of the plough as it covered their work. It would take the five of them a ten-hour day to plough and manure the acre.

'In California,' said the old man, 'they have ridges a mile long. With a four-row machine, those men would plant twenty acres a day.'

Next day, if the weather held, two of the men would break up the soil with mattocks, hacking here, chopping there, in steady progression from end to end of the field, furrow after furrow; and after them would come three men, each with one of the long narrow spades peculiar to the district, each with a sack of skiollauns fastened to his waist. Walking backwards, at each step they would drive the spade into the ground, push it forward, and drop the seed potato into the hole behind it. Three men abreast, right feet pressing on the spades, left hands on the handles levering the soil, right hands picking from the 'pouches' and dropping the skiollauns into their places.

When I went back to the kitchen, Patty Cronin had joined his wife. Had I seen the lights last night, he asked—the fairy lights? I had not, I said. 'Oh then, I seen them,' he said, 'and 'twas all on account of digging that hole in the old pathway. You should never disturb an old path.'

''Twas when he was going to bed he saw them,' said Kate, his wife.

''Twas when I was going to say me prayers I saw them,'

said Patty. 'I looked out of the window across the lake, and wasn't the whole of Denny's house lit up: every door and window was alive with lights. There's a power of people after arriving, I said to myself, for every room to be lit like that. And then I said me prayers and when I looked out the lights was still shining, and then as I made a small turn to get into bed, they all went out. 'Twas black dark again.'

'There was no one came and there was no lights there,' said Denny. 'John and myself was inside here in this back room, and there wasn't as much as a candle in the front.'

'Faith, he saw them all right,' said Kate.

'You should never disturb their path,' said Patty. 'Joan was coming home the other night and she said the place was alive with lights where they'd been digging.'

I mentioned the long narrow spade 'peculiar to the district.' Few people realize that the Irishman on his potato patch or in his bog is as particular about his spade or his slaun as a carpenter or a cabinet-maker might be about his chisels. By the very nature of the soil of Ireland, varying as it does from place to place, a specialized trade in shovel-making grew up and has survived through the years. In the south of Ireland alone there are close on a hundred patterns of spades, with about half that number of different shapes of slaun—light spades with a wing on them for cutting turf. Such districts in County Cork as Bantry, Ballydehob, Skibbereen, Dunmanway, and Bandon, all within an area not forty miles in greatest length, have their own particular design of spade, and a man from any one of them will scorn the implement preferred by his neighbours. Similarly with the slaun. A turf cutter from Killorglin or Killarney in Kerry can only use a blade with its wing on the left, whereas a worker from Kenmare in the same county will only use one with the wing on the right. I was told how, during the recent 'Emergency,' men from Cork, Limerick, and Clare, working side by side in a bog, were unable to use each other's slauns. In both spades and slauns there are minute differences in the splay of the blades as well as variations in the angle at which they are set on the handle. Some will be most suitable for soft, spongy turf, others for tougher banks. At Monard

Shovel Mills on the Blarney River near Cork, to call a spade a spade would be an insult. You must be precise. They can offer you a choice of two hundred and seventy varieties of spades and shovels, as well as from sixty to seventy slauns. For over two hundred years now these mills have carried on their craft almost without change. The same wheels are turned by the water; one of the original tilt hammers is still in use. Even the names of the workers have not changed: Willie and John Hayes belong to the sixth generation of that family, the O'Haras have been there for four generations. Their cottages, too, set in a wealth of laburnums, lilacs, and rhododendrons, are of an age with the tall trees that overhang the lake. The whole process is elemental—wind, water and fire working together to create the tools for the tilling of the land. Wind to fan the fires, water to drive the wheels, fire to heat the iron. Primitive methods have remained unaltered because there was no need to change them: the same tools are needed on the land. Inside the dark rock-walled caverns, figures move through the smoke; glowing metal is lifted from the furnaces, placed on the anvils, twisted and turned, cut and shaped under the rhythmic pounding of the great hammers. Heating, hammering, cooling, re-heating, hammering again—so the metal is 'drawn,' with the inevitable gestures of long custom. The glowing bar is lifted and swung, the tongs pass from acolyte to priest, and the sound of the hammer's pounding is like the thundering of a tremendous drum.

CHAPTER FIVE

THE BEST THING you could have is a Ford van,' said Mr. Morrissy of the C. A. B. Motor Company in Cork, when I consulted him one day about the purchase of a motor vehicle in which I could move about the country at leisure and sleep in if I so desired. 'Come and we 'll see Mr. O'Reilly,' he said.

In the works I explained to the two of them that speed didn't matter, that it was a movable shelter I needed with as much space in it as could be fitted on two ordinary pairs of wheels. Plenty of light inside was necessary, too, and a few bookshelves.

Mr. O'Reilly agreed with Mr. Morrissy's diagnosis. 'We 'll have it ready for you in three weeks,' said Jack O'Leary, who was to put the job in hand. And they did. On the day appointed I drove away from their headquarters, and Ireland lay before me. The fact that I nearly killed a policeman at the first corner didn't matter. 'I 'm sorry,' I said to him, 'but I 'm new to this car.' 'I could see that,' he said. ''Tis nothing at all!' So we parted friends.

It wasn't long before the passenger seat came into use. An old woman on the Carrigrohane road asked me for a lift. She said she was going three English miles to the west.

'You 'd be a native of these parts, I suppose?' she said as we went along.

'I am,' I said.

'And what would your name be, might I ask?'

I told her.

'Would you be a son of the minister was here a while back?'

'I would.'

'And aren't you a fine strong man, God bless you. Yerra, there's nothing like them Protestant clergy for bringing up families. Sure, aren't they decent, honest men, every one of them, and don't they set a fine example to their children. Oh then, I remember your father well—as quiet and sober a man as ever I met. 'Twas one day I boiled a kettle for him. His bicycle was after breaking down on the road, and he was dry for a cup of tea. "Are them all your children?" says he. "They are indeed, your reverence," says I. I had two of them talking, and another one walking, and another in the cradle and another one coming. "I dunno would they eat a sweet," says he, and with that out of his pocket he pulls a whole bag of sweets and gives them to the children. 'Twasn't often he came that way, but ever after he never passed the door without leaving in a bag of buns or maybe biscuits for the children.'

No other great events happened until I reached Ballingeary. There to the north of the bridge, by the little stream, I found Paddy the Forge banding wheels. I pulled the van in beside James Corkery's store and stopped to watch proceedings.

'Begod, you're free as a tinker now,' said Paddy as he inspected the van.

He had had to wait eleven days before he could be sure of a day when the rain wouldn't quench his fire. Two and a quarter inches wide by three-quarters of an inch thick, each iron band. A fortnight earlier he had measured their lengths by putting a chalk mark on the rim of each wheel and rolling it along the metal. Then, with an extra inch and a half for the welded joint, he had cut the lengths and bent them in a clamp into circles that were at least as geo-metrically accurate as the wheels supplied to him by Shaun Carroll the carpenter. 'You wouldn't be out by as much as the black of your nail,' Paddy told me. Now Danny, his

assistant, was piling turf on the ring of fire in which the bands were being heated.

Paddy was in reflective mood. He had nothing to do but rest on the stock of one of the wheels that lay on the ground, waiting till the metal was hot enough for action.

'Danny seems a fine boy,' I said.

'He is then,' said Paddy, 'a damn fine steady lad and a great worker. And I 'll tell you this,' he added, 'he 's a very different man to one of the same name that was with me a while back, Danny Mac we called him. He was the divil with the bellows, but he wasn't one small piece of good with the sledge. And about once a month he 'd start play-acting—'twould be when he had a bit of money coming to him. "There 's someone inside of the bellows," he 'd say. "I can hear him," he 'd say. And then he 'd run away out of the door with the fright. And then he 'd come back, and he 'd begin again at the bellows, and he 'd say: "Would it be a fairy, do you think? He 's booing and he 's hooing! I be afraid to stay here," he 'd say. And then he 'd run away out to the door, and then he 'd run away back, and then he 'd run away out altogether and I wouldn't see him again for a week. He 'd go and drive a spree till he hadn't a penny left of what he 'd earned.'

Paddy cut a fill of tobacco for his pipe, and lit it.

'D' ye know,' he said, 'I 'll be getting the pension next week, and there 's a year and a half of it back is due to me. 'Tis the only time in my life I ever saved a penny and that was done for me, for with all the to-ing and the from-ing I couldn't get a hold of it before, and now there 's a little bit of an accumulation. But I tell you,' he said, 'I won't keep it long, either, for I don't hold with keeping it. Amn't I right?' he asked.

I agreed with him.

'I tell you what,' he said. 'We 'll get hold of Batty Kit and we 'll go off in your van and we 'll make a day of it, and what 's more, if you can't drive home in the evening we 'll stay over the night and come back the day after.'

To this I didn't agree quite so heartily.

Meanwhile, in the intervals of putting on turf, Danny had filled two buckets with water from the nearby stream and rolled an unshod wheel on to the metal plate, embedded in the ground, that served as an operating table. This plate, a relic of an armoured car from the 'Anglo-Irish war,' had a circular hole cut in it to receive the stock of the wheel. With the aid of a few old spade blades as wedges, the wheel would lie flat and level. Close beside the plate was a large stone that could be used as an anvil, and close to the stone was a pool of the river into which the finished wheel would be dropped to contract the metal and give it a tighter grip on the timber.

There were sixteen wheels to be done and four of their bands were now in the fire. Jim the Spring—there 's a wonderful well beside his house—came and joined us. A pair of his wheels were among the sixteen; they were forty-two years old and these were the last bands they would carry. He just only wanted a bit of metal that would see them out.

'What 's the news?' he asked as he sat down.

'Ah, Wall Street is very low,' said Paddy.   As he spoke he winked at me.

'Walled streets?' asked Jim.   'Where would they be?'

'New York,' said Paddy.

'And for what would they be low?'

''Tis the bulls and the bears,' said Paddy.

'The bulls and the bears?' said Jim, mystified.

'They do be fighting each other,' said Paddy.   'If it's a bull that's on top the bear hasn't got a chance, and if it's a bear the bull might as well eat his own tail.'

'Is it a menagerie you're talking about?' said Jim.

'Begod, it's something very like, only a bit wilder and more senseless,' said Paddy.   By this time he had exhausted his knowledge of finance and wished to change the subject. 'Danny!' he called.   'Put a bit more on to the west there.' He got up himself to take the shovel.

'Haven't he great learning?' said Jim to me.

'There's no man knows more about his job,' I said.

'Walled streets, walled streets,' mused Jim.   'Sure, isn't that ancient history?'

'About a hundred and fifty years,' I said.

'One hundred and fifty?' said Jim.   'Arrah, man! There's a stone in my wall with the writing on it that's more than one thousand and fifty years old.   'Twas a man from the college in Cork came to see it and, says he, 'twas there before St. Patrick brought the faith.'

And now with the light breeze to fan it and no sun to quieten it the fire had done its duty.   Danny poured a bucket of water over the wheel that lay ready for its band.   That would prevent it catching fire when the hot metal was applied.   With iron clamps, known as draggers, the two men lifted one of the bands from the fire and carried it to the wheel, dropping it with one side in place against the timber.

Then using the other ends of the same clamps Danny got a grip on the unfitted edge, levering and straining as if to stretch it. And while he did this Paddy with a heavy sledge kept hammering the remainder to a closer fit. It was only a matter of moments before, with a good stroke of the sledge on its side, the band dropped into place. A few taps here and there and then, with much hissing and spluttering, into the pool went the completed job. Three more bands were put on their wheels, four more were put in the fire to redden and the turf heaped over them.

'Come on over to Shorten's,' said Paddy. 'That heat would put a drought in you.'

When we reached the pub there was an old friend of mine standing outside, a man well known in the neighbourhood, especially for his singing. *Red is the Rose* is his favourite song, and on a Saturday night in the bus from Cork he usually has a large, if enforced, audience. But this time he was solitary and in more contemplative than musical mood. He was standing there looking at a shilling that lay in the palm of his

hand. He had apparently spent quite a few similar coins on
the other side of the door, and this was the only one that now
remained.

'What will I do with you?' he kept repeating. 'What will
I do with you? Will I take you home with me or will I
drown you?' At last, coming to a decision, he said: 'I think
I 'll drown you,' and so saying he went inside.

We followed him into the house. Tim Harrigan, a lorry
driver from Macroom, was telling about a thunderstorm that
had flooded Cork the day before. 'The drains was busted,'
he said, 'and the rats was coming up like bubbles, as big as
cats they were, and with the power of the water the iron caps
of the manholes was floating about, two feet above the
street level.'

'And with the glass so high!' said the girl behind the
counter.

'Don't pay any attention to the glass,' said Paddy, ''tis no
good up here. The weather doesn't hold with it. Pay
attention to your bones, 'tis them will tell you the weather
that 's coming.'

A large car with a man and a woman in it passed slowly by
the open door of the pub.

'I think she 's bad still,' said Tim Harrigan.

'She 's a pity, the poor thing,' said Paddy. 'Sure, after all
the bombing he brought her over from England and put her
down in a farm of sixty acres, east of Macroom. He thought
'twas the way it would quieten the nerves. And what good
was it to her? If she as much as put her foot in a bit of cow's
dung on the road, she 'd be shaking for a fortnight.'

'There 's a man up at Gougane now, and he 's bad with
nerves,' I said. 'He 's going round with a nurse.'

''Tisn't nerves,' said Paddy, 'it 's money, too much
money. He 's afraid he 'll lose a penny of it. And if he did

he'd be the better off for it, for he'd get sleep at night, and isn't that riches to any man?' He put his glass down on the table and ordered another round.

'Saving, saving,' he continued. 'What good is that? I'd rather spend a two-shilling piece in a goblet of one of them bottles up there than to be leaving it behind me. And what value do it keep? Two shillings to-day, twopence to-morrow, and the day after no more than a farthing.'

'Excuse me, sir, but are you the famous orauthor?' said an elderly stranger who was sitting on the bench. 'They tell me you've journeyed the universe. Were you ever in Clonakilty?'

'"Clonakilty—God help us!"' exclaimed Paddy.

'"One teapot in the town and that without a spout,"' said Harrigan.

'Don't believe a word of it,' said the stranger. 'Every house in the town has a teapot of its own, and some of them are damn fine ones, too. I'm going back there to-morrow.'

'How are you travelling?' asked Paddy.

'Begor, I don't know, maybe I'd get a lift in the Posts and Telegraphs for part of the way anyway.'

'I'm going to Kinsale myself,' I said, 'and if a lift as far as Dunmanway or Bandon would help you——'

'What time will you be starting?' he asked.

'Early,' I said. 'Nine o'clock I'll be passing.'

'As sure as my name's Mick Brady,' he said, 'I'll be waiting for you.'

At this juncture Danny came to tell us that the iron was red. No, he wouldn't have anything to drink—he never touched it. Paddy went back with him to the fire, and I put the car on the straight road that winds its way to Gougane.

CHAPTER SIX

MICK BRADY WAS WAITING for me next morning
at the forge. I judged him to be about seventy years of age.
Though his body was supple his face was weathered, and when
he lifted his hat there wasn't a blade between the tips of his
ears and heaven. When he spoke the corners of his mouth
went up and down, first one side and then the other; his
eyebrows, too, and the tip of his short nose twitched like a
rabbit's. Though he spoke with solemnity it seemed that at
any moment, in spite of himself, he might burst into laughter.

As we drove along the road beside the Inchigeelah lakes,
we could see moorhens gathering material for their nests
among the tasselled reeds and swans on islets piling up dead
rushes in readiness for their eggs. A corncrake was calling
from a meadow. Celandines and kingcups outshone the gorse.

Mick said to me: 'My father's sister lived a mile to the
north of us here. She married a man by the name of
Scanlan. His mother came from Gougane and 'twas one
evening when she was travelling west by the lake—there was
no road there then, only a little bit of a track—she looked in

the lake and what did she see but fields of corn and sheep and every sort of land and crop and stock. She was an old woman at the time and she knew well enough 'twas a kind of an enchantment must be on the lake, so says she to herself, if I can keep an eye on it all and throw in a bit of iron at it the spell will be broken. So she kept her eyes fixed on the fields and the cattle and the pigs and the hens, and all the time she was thinking where would she get a bit of iron. And the only bit she could think of was in the heel of her shoe. 'Twould be worth it to throw in the shoe, says she. But when she went to unrip the lace wasn't it tangled in a knot, and for the glint of a second she took her eye off the land. When she looked again 'twas all disappeared and the lake was there the same as ever.'

Our road turned south, through a wilderness of rock and bog and lilied pools.

'My brother's wife's brother lives west behind that hill,' said Mick. 'Tom Sweeney is his name. His wife died, and two years after he married another girl, a fine girl she was. But the night of the wedding, when she got into bed, didn't the first wife come into the room, and didn't she lay her two cold hands on the face of the one in the bed.'

Now the road was taking us through a valley rich with the deep green of grazing lands and the pale green of young corn.

'There's a cousin of mine lives east in that farm,' said Mick. 'He married a woman ten years older than himself. She's that mean that every penny she gets she makes a prisoner of it. The friction is hot and strong between the two of them. I tell you, when he gets away from her he's like a lamb lepping.'

'You seem to have a lot of relations,' I remarked.

'I'm related to a fright of people,' he said. 'I have thousands of people related to me, and some of them was poets. Haven't poets a great power of words?' he added thoughtfully. 'There was a poet stopped all the corn and grass growing in Leinster with the blast of his words because the men of Leinster had killed his son. Sure, 'tis well known they could rhyme a man to death.'

Mick was right in this. An old record states that 'in A.D. 1414, John Stanley, the Deputy of the King of England, arrived in Ireland, a man who gave neither mercy nor protection to clergy, laity, or men of science, but subjected as many of them as he came upon to cold hardship and famine. It was he who plundered Niall, the son of Hugh O'Higgins. The O'Higgins, with Niall, then satirized John Stanley, who lived after this satire but five weeks, for he died of the virulence of the lampoons.' Many similar cases are on record, some of them not very reputable, as when a queen of Connaught, in love with a poet, offered him the kingdom. 'How can that be with the king living?' said the poet. 'It is an easy matter,' replied the queen, 'for you are a poet, and can bring a blemish on his cheek. A man with a blemish cannot enjoy the kingdom.' And so it came about.

'When I was a young man,' continued Mick, 'I knew hundreds of poems. Listen to me now, did you ever hear this one:

> ' " Much I 've heard about the Rhine,
>   With vineyards gay and castles stately;
>   But those who think I care for wine
>   Or lofty towers, mistake me greatly:
>   A thousand times more dear to me
>   Is whiskey by the silvery Lee." '

'Could you write it down for me?' I asked, stopping the car and offering him paper and pencil.

'You scratch while I give tongue,' he said.

E

We had hardly got under way again before he said: 'Do you know *The Cruiskeen Lawn*? That 's a damn fine song.'

The song had many verses and a chorus, and each time with the chorus there had to be a long and a warm shake hands. It didn't matter whether we were going round a sharp corner or were among a herd of straying cattle, I had to put my right hand across the steering-wheel and allow it to be shaken violently while he sang:

> '"Gra-ma-chree ma cruiskeen
> Slainte geal mavourneen
> Gra-ma-chree a coolin bawn bawn bawn
> Gra-ma-chree a coolin bawn." '

the gist of which is:

> 'My heart's love is my little jug,
> Bright health to my darling.'

After I had nearly taken the tail from one of a flock of Aylesbury ducks, 'with bellies on 'em like majors' as Mick put it, he began to chant:

> '"The dear little fellow, his legs they were yellow,
> He 'd fly like a swallow, he 'd swim like a hake,
> Till some wicked savage to grease his white cabbage
> Went and murdered Nell Flaherty's beautiful drake."'

And then with tremendous enthusiasm:

> '"May his pig never grunt, may his cat never hunt,
> That a ghost may catch him in the dark of the night,
> May his hen never lay, may his ass never bray,
> And his goat fly away like an old paper kite."'

From hungry slopes of barren land we dropped into a valley red with earth prepared for sowing, green with springing corn. Willows apple-green with leaf, and willows gold with blossom, lined the banks of streams heavy with drifts of water crow's-foot.

It was when we came in sight of Dunmanway that he recited:

> '"'Tis there the lake is, where duck and drake is,
>   And the crane can take his sweet meal of frogs;
>   But when night comes round it, the spirits surround it,
>   For there was drownded Sir Richard Cox."

You see,' he said, 'that wasn't the Sir Richard Cox that was the lord chancellor justice, or something like that, of all Ireland. 'Twasn't his son, neither. Maybe 'twas his grandson, but I couldn't be sure. Anyway, he was a poor sort of a fellow, with more in his pocket than in his head, and 'twas the time when a man by the name of John Wesley came preaching to Ireland. He was a great missioner, I 'm told, and there 's many prays like him to-day. I 'm not rightly sure whether 'twas himself or one of his preachers was coming to Dunmanway, but whoever he was the young Sir Richard didn't like the idea and thought he 'd give him a ducking in the lake. So he gets hold of a boat, the day before, and he takes it out on the lake just to practise, and didn't the boat upset and himself get pinned underneath and drowned. And do you know, the water was that shallow he could have walked ashore on his knees.'

'Wasn't it a wonder no one tried to save him?' I asked.

'There was a black cloud came down on the lake,' said Mick, 'and they were all affrighted to go near him.'

As he opened his coat to look for his pipe I saw a row of medals on the inside of his jacket.

'You 're well decorated,' I said to him.

'Begor, I am,' he said, pulling back the other side of the jacket and disclosing an array of religious medals. 'Them on the left is for the wars I 'm after winning in this world, and them on the right is to keep me out of wars in the next world.'

By the time we reached Dunmanway I had decided that as it was only another dozen miles to Clonakilty I might as well take the old man the whole way to his home and then find my way to Kinsale along the coast, so we continued south through the town and along the road towards the sea.

Some few generations ago, when this district was more isolated and lawsuits were even more protracted and tedious than at the present day, the inhabitants devised some pretty ways of summary justice. For instance, if a man would not pay a debt, the creditor served him with what was called 'a fairy process'; in other words, he stole his cow, his horse, or other animals whose value would be equivalent to the money owing. So well was this understood that, if a man at any time should find some of his stock missing, he would seek out his creditor and settle the account. Next morning, much to his surprise of course, he would find all his animals grazing again in their own fields.

In that district, too, they had a simple way of keeping accounts between employer and labourer. A stout stick,

two or three feet long, would be split down its centre to within a few inches of one end, at which point one of the sections would be separated from the remainder. When accounts had to be 'entered,' the two pieces were held together in their original position and notches in the form of a St. Andrew's cross cut at their junction. Each cross represented eight days' work. The employer retained the piece with the handle, the labourer keeping the portion cut off. A straight line cut in the stick after a series of crosses denoted that all work up to that mark had been paid for.

Dunmanway is a friendly town, so is Clonakilty. By the time I'd said good-bye to Mick I felt that I knew every one in 'Clon' and they knew everything about me.

It had been my intention to reach Kinsale before night-fall, but at Timoleague the tide was low and the mudflats in the estuary shimmered in the sun. Curlews and oyster-catchers were there in flocks, shelducks in pairs, and herons stalking their solemn solitary courses. I stopped the van and watched a curlew probing in a pool among some rocks close to the shore. Here and there it explored with the tips of its part-opened bill. Then, deep down, it sensed some morsel. It drove its bill deeper, closing its eyes as the water almost covered its head; then with a good tug it brought to the surface its booty tangled in green weed. The bird shook it, passed it from side to side of the tip of its bill, shook it again, then with a jerk threw it back across the angle of the bill. One bite and the weed fell away; one gulp and the morsel was swallowed.

As I followed the road to Coolmain I saw a lorry emerging from some sandhills. If that can travel in such terrain, I said to myself, this van can do the same, so, following the track that led me first through shallow water and then across firm sand, I reached the dunes. Beyond them and across another stretch of sand was the sea, thin lines of glittering foam, almost lost in haze, edging the ocean that was luminous as a crystal and smooth as if ironed by the heat of the day. The last lorry was leaving, piled high with sand; there wasn't a human being in sight. There was no reason why I should go further.

CHAPTER SEVEN

WITH THE SETTING of the sun the wind dropped, and the sand seemed warmer to the feet. Shoeless I sat among the dunes, listening to the last notes of the whinchats in the gorse near by, watching the last flutterings of pipits above the bents and rushes. Rabbits emerged from their burrows or from their forms in the marram grass, scampering here and there erratically, never in a straight line like a hare, leaving their record of travel in a code of dashes and dots, two long, two short, the hind ones always ahead because of the leap-frog action in the animal's gait.

While delighting in the sand about my feet and the multitudinous gem-like grains of it that poured through my fingers, the sad thought came to me that, however much we exult in such things, however much we yearn to be skin-close to these realities, it is only with tired feet on hot pavements that many of us can find achievement. But that was no place for thoughts of cities. Instead I recalled the sand dunes behind Hurghada on the Egyptian coast of the Red Sea, vast elemental forms sculptured by the wind, in ranks across the desert. The sand there is ever shifting, there are no grasses to stay its course. The dunes move as the wind listeth to blow.

Across the Red Sea on the slopes of Sinai is Jebel Nakus, or the Hill of the Bell, a high sandstone ridge in which, within a crescent of rocks, is sand piled to a height of about three hundred feet. When disturbed either by the wind or by footsteps, there emerge from this sand sounds which have been variously described as like those of a humming-top, an Aeolian harp, or a church bell; and all of which, with further disturbance of the sand, increase in volume until they rival the rumbling of distant thunder. It seems to be thought by scientists to-day that the sounds are produced by vibrations set up in the air when the sand rolls slowly down from the summit. The Arabs, however, believe that the musical strains come from the bells of a convent long buried in the sand. Whatever the explanation, this is by no means the only instance of its kind. Similar music may be heard at the hill of Regh Rawan, about forty miles north of Kabul in Afghanistan, which many Mohammedans believe to be the place where their long-awaited Iman Medi will appear upon earth; and in the Great Gobi Desert one may still hear 'the sound of a variety of musical instruments, and still more commonly the sound of drums' as described by Marco Polo after he had traversed that region nearly seven hundred years ago.

It was when reading a modern account of the Gobi Desert that I learned of the many ways in which the long desert grass of otherwise barren tracts can be used by the inhabitants. It reminded me of the coco-nut palm in Polynesia which fills almost every need of the islanders, from the building of their houses to the rearing of their infants. In the Gobi, the grass when young is used for fodder; as it grows tougher it is knotted into nets to hold back the sand, and hurdles to restrain the stock. Like the fronds of the palm, it is woven into mats and baskets. Like the fibres of the coco-nut husk, it is woven into cord and rope. Like the midrib of the coco-nut frondlets, the stalks of the grass are used for brushes. In Polynesia the coco-nut palm can be used in more than a hundred ways; it would seem that the grass in the Gobi Desert can serve as many purposes.

In Ireland, except for occasional use as thatch or litter, the marram grass is scarcely used, being left to fulfil the more important function of sand-break. Some years ago in Dingle Bay, when a quantity of it had been cut, the sea 'made great irruptions.' Incidentally, but for the protection of marram grass on Spurn Head in Yorkshire, a large part of the city of Hull would no longer be in existence.

What with the music of Aeolian harps, humming-tops, and church bells in my ears, sleep overcame me early that night at Coolmain. Next morning I awoke at dawn. No breath of wind stirred the grasses. Lorry tracks and footprints had disappeared with the midnight tide. A thousand acres of the shore were mine. Seaward all was lost in haze, and when, as I waded through the shallows, I glanced behind me, the land too was screened from sight. It was a perfect morning for a mermaid to come ashore and comb her hair. She could have sat there in the shallow water with the sea a mirror all around her, and no one to disturb her. I wouldn't have tried to steal her head-dress and compel her to stay with me. What could I have done with her in the van? How could I have gone buying her clothes? How could she have gone buying them with nothing to wear? One must be practical. The towns in County Cork are very conservative and questions would almost certainly have been asked. It was in one of them that I was told: 'You must go and see Mrs. Dunston. She 's very broad-minded—she reads your books.'

It is a sad fact that in medieval times the mermaids became

confused with the sirens: in Homer's day the former were as benevolent as they were beautiful. Didn't Ino give her veil to Odysseus to save him from the wrath of Poseidon the sea-god? And in Homer's day, too, they didn't have fish tails. 'Ino of the Fair Ankles' obviously needed nothing of the kind. Fashions change and, with fashions, morals—or is it the other way about? The sea was too cold for me to stay in until I had reached a conclusion.

Inland the water was seeping from the mudflats and trickling through winding gulleys into the larger channels. Turnstones were flicking pebbles at the edge of the tidal stream, picking up sandhoppers, worms, and other luckless creatures. The surface of the mud was pied with shelduck seeking their sustenance. As I watched them they seemed to me, surely, the handsomest of all ducks, with their sturdy build, easy gait, and clearly defined black, white, and russet plumage. Then I remembered that the Pintail ducks, because of their elegance of shape and their delicacy of colouring, had once held first place in my affections, and that reminded me of the surpassing brilliance of the Paradise ducks I had seen in New Zealand. Again, I thought of my earliest love, the little black-and-white tufted duck, the most endearing of them all for its gaiety and apparent sense of humour. It is very difficult for an artist to be faithful. Whatever he is drawing must at that moment seem to him the most exquisite of its kind. Drawing is exploration, and the excitement of new discoveries weaves momentary spells. Few artists can keep the affairs of their minds in such happy order as the Cork man who said to me: 'The loveliest thing I 've seen in this world, after my wife, is Chartres.'

By now I had decided to go out of my course another few miles and visit Garrettstown strand near the Old Head of Kinsale. For the seven years that my father was rector of

Kinsale, Garrettstown was to us children the summit of our ambition for picnics. It was seven miles from the town, a long distance for small boys, but my mother would organize parties, hiring a two-horse waggonette for the occasion. 'Oh, boys, do you smell the sea?' she would say with delight, as we drove along the last mile of tree-shaded road that brought us to the strand. Then there would be paddling and bathing and the building of sand castles, and old Joaney who lived in a cottage on the cliff near by would boil kettles for our tea. My mother loved the wildness of that strand, not only in summer but in winter, and when in Kinsale after a south-westerly gale she could hear the distant rumble of the storm-flung shingle, she would hire a side-car and, taking a few of us with her, drive out 'to see the waves.' One of my clearest recollections of that strand is of her standing on the crown of the great wall of shingle, wrapped in a grey worsted cloak, while wave after wave lifted the stones and hurled them eastwards along the shore. After we left Kinsale and were living at Carrigrohane, twenty miles inland, the strand still held its attraction, and I would often go there alone on my bicycle, for the day. Then came a time when I had greater ambitions; I wanted to spend several days there and nights also, sleeping as close to the surf as possible. So I borrowed a donkey and cart and, loading a waterproof sheet and some blankets, set off. It wasn't long before I discovered that either the cart or the harness didn't fit the donkey, for whenever we were on a downhill slope the cart ran on the animal's hindquarters, and there was soon no hair left on its tail. It meant that from then on I had to walk downhill as well as uphill, and as there was very little flat country on my route I eventually did most of the twenty miles on foot. But after breaking the journey at a friend's house where the donkey was given a feed of oats and I was given a bed, we reached our destination late on the second evening. It was already growing dark when I knocked at Joaney's half door and asked if I might let the little ass loose in her field for the night.

'You can, to be sure,' she told me. 'And where will you put the cart?'

'Up against the bank,' I said. 'With the waterproof sheet thrown over the shafts I'll have a fine tent.'

And so I would if it hadn't come on to rain, and if the waterproof hadn't been an old one. Clouds had been gathering to the south-west before I lay down. Soon they were overhead, and soon the big drops that had begun to fall on my covering gathered themselves into rivulets which varied their descent upon my person according to the vagaries of the gale now blowing. Neither was the floor of the cart waterproof as I had hoped: increasing trickles came through on to my feet.

About midnight Joaney's daughter-in-law appeared, with a lantern, to see how I was getting on. She said that what with herself and her husband and the children and the grandmother in the cottage, it was a small piece crowded, but they'd just put the roof on a new hen-house, and even if the floor was a bit wet they had an old mattress they could lend me. So, gratefully, I moved in, and would no doubt have slept peacefully if the mattress hadn't been stored for some months before in the old hen-house. There is a pleasant oriental tale of a flea who, knowing that thieves were about to enter the palace, awakened his master the king by biting him, thus foiling the robbers' plans. It would have taken a skilful thief to rob me that night.

There is nothing left of Joaney's house to-day save one gable wall, but the same old bank is there with its lichen-covered stones facing to the sea and daisies and vetches on the sheltered side, and there's the same little bit of a dip close to the bank wherein I thought to take my rest.

This time there was no need for me to sleep under a bank for, apart from the van, there was a two-handed welcome from Mrs. O'Neill in the hotel that has since been built high up on the cliff. It couldn't be in a better position, sheltered from the north and east, looking west across the twin crescent bays of Garrettstown and the White Strand to the Old Head, and with the sea and cliffs a matter of yards to the south. Three days later I was still there.

One afternoon I wandered eastwards along the great rampart of pebbles behind the wide stretch of sand. Big waves were swinging in from the south-west, lifting the stones and throwing them high on the slope, obliquely towards the east, leaving them there to roll downwards again by their shortest course. It was easy to see how such banks of shingle are constantly in movement, their motion governed by prevailing winds.

When I reached the White Strand, half a mile to the east, numerous small birds were on the shore, busy among the sand-hoppers that had been disturbed by a tide rather higher than usual. A kestrel swooped at one of the birds, a pied wagtail. No aerial battle could have been fought with greater speed, both birds banking and twisting faster than my eyes could follow them. The skirmish lasted scarcely a minute and ended when the wagtail, coming low, glided under an upturned boat. As it did so the kestrel, catching sight of me, flew away. When I looked under the boat, two wagtails and half a dozen pipits which had been hiding there flew out.

CHAPTER EIGHT

KINSALE IS LIKE AN ancient oak forest whose topmost shoots have suffered with the years but whose roots are deep into the soil, and whose trunks and branches, rich with ferns and flowers and mosses, will never lose their character.

The town, whose first charter was granted by Edward III in 1333, stands at the head of an extensive harbour, encompassed by hills. Its houses are built along those hills, one above the other, so that there seems scarcely a basement that does not overlook an attic. No two houses are alike and it may be for that reason that their occupants also have an individuality of character. The town straggles and climbs. There are main streets in which two men on bicycles can scarcely pass. There are thoroughfares that for steps rival the Strada Stretta of Malta. And on all sides there are ruins of forts and castles: James Fort, 1601, a keep within its moat on the hill, and Charles Fort, 1670, whose bastions meet the water's edge, the two of them guarding the narrows between outer and inner harbours. There is a block house that once assisted the forts, and a mile or so up the River Bandon, which flows into the harbour, there is Ringroan Castle, not to mention many others. It is on record that after the Battle of Kinsale in 1601, the officers and men of Queen Elizabeth's army, to commemorate their victory over the Spanish troops, subscribed £700 to purchase books for the library of Trinity College, Dublin, which speaks well for the military of that time. Visitors to Trinity College will find over the stairs leading to the library a large painting of the Battle of Kinsale with an inscription concerning its special significance in that position.

Ringroan Castle, which belongs to the de Courcys, Lords Kingsale, is thought to have been built by them in the thirteenth century. With the nearby James Fort it was the scene of the last Williamite battle in Ireland, in September 1690. Nothing of that castle remains to-day but a single wall, standing like a great monolith on the hill. Fifty years ago there was another wall surviving. I remember it because it was there that, at the age of ten, I made my first attempt at sketching. With another boy, now a Very Revd., I crept away shyly, complete with notebook and pencil, and later in the day was not displeased by my parents' comments when I ventured to show them what I had done. This was my first practical adventure into the realms of art, though a year earlier when on holiday at Baltimore, a sea port some fifty miles from Kinsale, my eyes had been opened by a friend of my mother's who could do what seemed to me wonders with a box of water-colours. She must have been about thirty-five years of age and I was about nine, and I used to stand behind her for hours while she sketched, watching the miracles she worked on paper, watching, too, the lights in the rather prim coils of her flaxen hair. · I confessed to my mother that I would like to marry Emily, but she gently dissuaded me.

I do not remember any other great excursions into art at that time. My energies were too taken up in shivering at early morning bathing parties and sweating at midday bicycle picnics, for I was the youngest among my companions and I found it very hard to keep up with them.

At that time Kinsale was a prosperous town. Fishing-boats from Scotland, Cornwall, and the Isle of Man followed the herring and the mackerel in their courses, and during the week the quay would be alive with men and women salting and packing the fish, while at the week-end the inner harbour would be solid with smacks. At that time, too, a British regiment stationed in the town brought a considerable revenue to the business community. Now the fish have changed their feeding-grounds and the troops have departed, and the town has gone quietly and peacefully to sleep.

'Ah, but isn't it grand to be together again, after all the troubles?' said an elderly woman to me on Denis's Quay. 'Yerra, never mind the barracks. Sure, it brought great money to some, but what good was it to others? And what harm is it, too, if the fishing is gone? 'Tis a pity, surely, but no matter. D' you remember the way we 'd walk across the harbour on the decks of the smacks? 'Twas PL this and PL that, from Peel in the Isle of Man, and they 'd be anchored over by the Lower Road. They 'd be the first to arrive in March for the mackerel fishing, and then the Scotch boats would come for the herring in May, and they 'd anchor beyond by the pier, and the Cornish boats would be in in August for the harvest mackerel. 'Tis over at the Scilly Dam some of them would be, and they had PZ on their bows for

Penzance, or maybe SS for St. Ives, I think. And now the harbour is empty. Three lobster boats at the pier head and what would they get—maybe a few dozen of a night. And all the gentry are going or gone. Well, I suppose no man can live for ever. Sure, the old General above on the hill was ninety-three when he went, and the Captain below in the town was eighty-seven. But tell me, isn't it a lovely harbour? Did you ever see nicer in all your travels? No! I 'm thinking you never did. There 's some visitors be talking of the smell at low tide, but what 's a bit of a smell. Sure 'tis only from the mud and what would mud be if it hadn't a bit of a smell. And don't I know and don't you know many the fine hearty man and girl was brought up on those smells, and, sure, isn't it all washed by the sea twice every day, and how could it do harm. There was a priest came here last year, from Italy he was, and, says he, there 's no tides in the ocean around Italy at all, and when he seen the tide go out and leave the mud all bare, and then the tide to come in again and flood up to the doors of the houses without ever entering in: "Isn't it wonderful," says he, "the law and order of the Almighty?" '

We were standing on the edge of the quay, and before us was as nice a stretch of aromatic slob as you could ask to see or smell. Slime-covered ropes, chains, and cables led to half-sunken anchors or to yachts and row-boats lying on the worm-blistered mud. But the tide was rising and soon the same landscape would be transformed, its sheltered waters reflecting the erratic architecture of the town.

I had only fifty yards to walk to the house of an old friend, now a retired admiral. The bell wouldn't ring, the knocker seemed to have no effect on the household. The hall door was wide open, and I could have walked off with a pair of silver candelabra. Instead, I used the knocker a second time, more forcibly. The only reply was the opening of a window above my head. As I hadn't seen the admiral for forty years, and had never met 'his lady,' I didn't look up. Next moment a girl came hurtling down the stairs. She might have been the aunt of hers with whom I was in love at the age of twelve.

'Come in, come in!' she said. 'I'm father's daughter.'

'But you don't know who I am,' I said.

'I do,' she said. 'I put my head out of the window and I said to mother: "There's a man below at the door." "It's Bob Gibbings," she said.'

'How did she know?' I asked.

'She's like that,' said the daughter.

At that moment her mother sailed in looking not unlike a stately ship that had weathered a storm. Her clothes were in ribbons. I was only conscious of shreds and streamers held together with pins and tackings of white thread.

'Pat is fitting me with a new dress,' she said.

The admiral appeared soon after, and he was followed by others of the family. We discussed old times in Kinsale, the model yacht regatta which my mother organized each year for the young people, and the Saturday-night prayer meetings which my father organized when the fishing fleets were in the harbour. There was one old man at those meetings who always prayed. He invariably sat as far back in the hall as he could, until inspiration came: then he would move into the central aisle, drop on his knees, and begin to pray in a reverberating voice which steadily increased in volume. As he spoke he would work his arms backwards and forwards with a breast-stroke swimming action, and while he did so he would be slowly moving forward on his knees. We boys knew that there would be no release until he met the platform.

F

'Tell me,' said the admiral, 'why was it your father didn't like the idea of your becoming an artist?'

'Naked women,' I said. 'He thought I'd have to spend the rest of my life among them.' And then I told him how, years later, when the *Studio* reproduced a few of my engravings, I sent a copy of the magazine to my sister. 'Merciful Heaven!' she said when she opened it. 'There's a girl with nothing on.' 'Oh my, my,' said my father. 'What will the poor boy come to?'

From the admiral I went to see Miss Harrie Orr who had given me my very first lessons in drawing. 'Why, Bobby darling! is that yourself?' she said, throwing her arms round me and kissing me. We talked of my early efforts to copy geometric patterns, and of the school upstairs run by her sister Miss Eleanor, and then the subject changed to the old ladies who refused to bathe from the same beach as myself and my brother—'great big boys of ten and twelve,' and thence to the girl who swam across the harbour with a shoal of porpoises gambolling near, and from her to the two girls who always played hockey in dresses with long trains. Finally of the spinster to whom my mother lent the rectory while we were on holiday. With the house and garden was also lent my pet duck, but when I got home after a month's absence there was no sign of Winnie. I was told that she had 'died.'

'Now,' said Harrie when I was leaving, 'go down to the Castle Bar, 'tis no more than a few steps, and say a word to Mrs. Coleman. She remembers you.'

'If it isn't Bobby Gibbings himself,' said Mrs. Coleman from behind the bar as I went in. 'You don't remember me?' she said. 'But didn't I teach you your sums on a slate! Sure, I was Nora Crowley then, and I helped Miss Eleanor with her school.'

'Would you be any relation of Commander Gibbings?' asked a fisherman who was standing by the counter.

'A brother, probably,' I said.

'He commanded my ship in the first war, and faith when he heard I came from Kinsale I couldn't go wrong. When you see him tell him McCarthy was asking for him. Tell him I was in the last war, and tell him I was in the Merchant Navy in between wars and now I'm fishing—netting for salmon. I lost two of my sons in the last war,' he added.

Another fisherman dropped in. 'Torpedo,' they called him—'Torpedo Tim.' He had been a bar steward in a cross-channel service during the first war and three times his ship had been sunk. When it happened for the third time, the crash came as he was locking up for the night. 'Got us again!' he muttered to himself. So he pulled out the till, stuffed the whole of its contents into his trouser pockets, and rushed on deck just as the ship took a lurch and sank. He hadn't had time to fasten his lifebelt and as he went down it hit him under the jaw, breaking most of his teeth. 'I came up spitting blood and teeth—I hadn't a tooth left in me head. I haven't one now,' he told me.

After he had been picked up and landed he was sent to hospital where they wanted to undress him and put him to bed. Not very likely! Nobody was going to take *those* trousers from him. Oh, very well, if he didn't want to go to bed he could go home, they said. So he was sent home, and the first thing his wife wanted to do was to put her poor shipwrecked mariner to bed. Again the value of those trousers recurred to him. 'He's gone queer in the brain with the blast,' said his wife. Not until he had the money safely hidden did he recover his sanity.

Next day I couldn't resist a visit to Thuillier's boat-building yard. As a boy I used to watch racing yachts growing out of a foam of shavings on his father's pier; as a young man I used to hire yachts from him for a couple of shillings a day. Now there was no sign of sail-cloth, masts, or spars, but a brand-new dinghy rested on the grass awaiting its owner. In the shed alongside the pier another dinghy was in course of construction, many of its copper nails not yet riveted. Behind its newly planed, shining timbers of spruce there lay at the back of the shed an ancient bicycle— 'A boneshaker made by my father in '69,' said Mr. Thuillier. 'He modelled it in wood and then he took it along to Taed Murphy the blacksmith for the iron. Seventy-five pounds the whole thing weighed. But look at these,' he said, pointing to two 'penny-farthings' thrown in a corner. 'We got them from the police; they tried them for a time but they were too conspicuous. Sure, a helmet on the top of one of them would be seen for miles. But they were lovely things to ride; they 'd just glide off a stone if you met one. It was a beautiful sensation.'

Kinsale has produced many celebrated people, from Anne Bonny the pirate queen downwards. One gentleman of whom I have not spoken is Patrick Cotter O'Brien the giant, who was born in the neighbourhood in the year 1761. He died in Bristol at the age of forty-seven and was buried in the crypt of St. Joseph's Church in that city. As a boy, Cotter O'Brien was apprenticed to a stonemason, but he soon began to specialize in plastering ceilings, which thanks to his height he could do without the help of ladders. But a sudden change in his career occurred at the age of eighteen when a travelling showman agreed to pay his parents fifty pounds a year for his 'use.' There is no record of what Cotter was to get out of the bargain, but we may infer that it was limited, for it wasn't long before he left the showman and set up in a similar business on his own. By this time his imagination seems to have been in no way inferior to his physique, for on one of his handbills is printed:

> 'Just arrived in Town, and to be seen in a commodious room at No. 11 Haymarket, nearly opposite the Opera House, the celebrated Irish Giant, Mr. O'Brien of the Kingdom of Ireland, indisputably the tallest man ever shown. He is a lineal descendant of the old puissant King Brien Boreau, and has in person and appearance all the similitude of that great and grand Potentate. It is remarkable of this family that however various the revolutions in point of fortune and alliance, the lineal descendants thereof have been favoured by Providence with the original size and stature which have been so peculiar to their family. The Gentleman alluded to measures near nine feet high.
>
> ADMITTANCE ONE SHILLING.'

He forgot to mention that his immediate forbears in Kinsale were of normal size. However, his finger ring of gold, measuring one inch and a quarter in diameter and bearing many devices, was in the possession of a friend of mine, the late Henry Daunt of Kinsale, to whose grand-uncle in Bristol it had been given by O'Brien; and one of the giant's shoes, fifteen and a half inches in length, is to be seen in the Kinsale Museum.

CHAPTER NINE

'DO YOU SEE THE WAY the finger is stiff? I'll tell you how it happened, and it won't take two words to tell you.'

Pat Egan was standing beside a small fishing-boat drawn up on the ferry slip at what is known in Kinsale as the World's End. He was whittling some new thole pins with his penknife, fitting them from time to time in the holes in the gunwale. A man of about fifty, he wore a sailor's peaked cap and a navy-blue jersey knitted with an elaborate pattern of cable stitch. His face was as tanned as the sail that lay in the boat, and when he became solemn, and the wrinkles about his eyes smoothed out, there was a radiation of fine white lines from the outer corners of his eyes.

'Myself and Jim Barrett was going fishing—you didn't know Jim—he was away most of his time in the Merchant Navy. God Almighty, the stories that man had to tell, you'd forget to put bait on your hooks, and the two of us was east at the pier steps, and I was putting a stitch in the tack of the sail and Jim was putting a bit of hoop iron on the blade of an old oar he'd found floating. And old Jerry Long was there, he's buried since, the kindliest man I ever knew. There's some have their hands out to know what they can

get: he 'd have his hands out to know what he could give.
And a great man behind a horse—you knew him, he used to
drive for Acton's; haven't they a fine hotel there now on the
quay? And says Jerry, "Where are ye off to next, Jim?"
"New York," says Jim. "For long?" says Jerry. "Long
as your name," says Jim. "Wouldn't you be at sea in a
city?" says Jerry. "'Twould be water off a rhinoceros's
back," says Jim. "Begod, the hide on you is thick enough,
anyway," says Jerry. Sure, don't I remember every word
they said. 'Twas the way they 'd always be having gas with
each other.'

'I dunno will the ferry be going soon,' said a woman's
voice beside us.

'Wisha, Mary, how are you?' said Pat.

'I 'm pegged out,' she said.

'And how is Ned?'

'Yerra, he 's grand, thank God, sitting up outside in the
sun.'

'They told me he was near gone.'

'Sure, didn't the doctor say he was finished, and to let him
go easy and not be bothering him with the medicines, and
didn't the priest come and anoint him.'

Mary, a big stout woman, leaned her weight on the upper
gunwale of the boat, which immediately heeled over on to
its other side.

'Well,' she said, sighing, 'the trouble I had. Isn't death a
great upset?'

''Tis a change, anyway, for them that dies,' said Pat.

'Yerra, man, what with the papering of the room and the
getting in the bit of coal and the candles and the bottles of
liquor, I was destroyed.'

'And all for nothing,' said Pat.

'Wisha, 'twas a great fright he had. "Mary," says he to

me, "Mary," he says, "when death waves his hat at you there 's only the one answer." '

'And wasn't he wrong after all?'

'Sure, isn't he always wrong, the poor fellow.'

The ferry came in and bore Mary across to Castle Park and her miscalculating husband.

'I was telling you about the finger,' said Pat.

'We were down at the pier,' I said, 'with Jerry Long and Jim Barrett.'

'We were,' he said, 'and as I was putting the last stitch in the sail Johnny Cogan came along. You know Johnny— 'twas him was talking to you last night over at the salmon nets. Didn't they have a bad day yesterday? Two fish to one boat in the morning, and not another between the five of them for the rest of the day.'

'One of them had luck last week?' I suggested.

'Twenty-two fish in the last haul of the day, after a week with nothing,' said Pat. ''Twas the first haul after the low tide, and that and the last before it is the best.'

Salmon fishing is carried on from the shore between Scilly and Summer Cove on the north side of the harbour. Five boats are licensed and they work in strict rotation. Number two doesn't leave the shore till number one has finished its haul, likewise number three after number two, and so on. Five men to each boat. One of the crew, standing at the water's edge, holds the shore rope while the others rowing in a wide semicircle pay out the net as they go. Then, ashore, in their oilskin aprons and thigh-boots they begin to haul, two men on the head rope at the upper edge of the net, one on the foot rope, one gathering the mesh, 'the sleeve,' between the two. Nearly a hundred fathoms of it to be brought in, slowly, steadily, hand over hand. As the half circle of corks on the surface grows smaller the man on the shore rope walks slowly along the beach to join the others, dragging his end of the net with him. Hand over hand the hauling goes on, monotonously, almost as if the men were working in their sleep, the rhythm broken only to remove an occasional crab or starfish from the meshes. The ring of corks gets smaller and smaller; the last fold of the net, 'the bunt,' comes ashore: more often than not there is nothing in it.

'As I was telling you,' said Pat, 'Johnny Cogan came along. "Where are ye going?" says he. "The Crooked Ditch," says Jim. "How many lines have ye?" says Johnny. "Plenty," says Jim. "I 'll come with ye," says Johnny. So we pushed off from the pier and there wasn't the fill of your pipe of wind, but we crept along and just inside the mouth of the harbour we let down our lines. 'Twas plaice and dabs we were after but 'twas gurnard we were catching, and Jim was making us laugh with his stories of foreign parts. "The flying fish would come aboard like this," says he, swinging a red gurnard over the gunwale into my lap. Well, with the laughter that was on us, when I went to take it off the hook didn't a spine from its back go into me finger. Look, man, you can see the spot there on the joint,' he said, holding up his hand. 'From that day to this I never bent the finger. 'Twas maybe the way a bit of the spine broke off inside.'

CHAPTER TEN

'I SEEN A SNAIL on the road as I come along,' said Patty Cronin, 'a black snail with grey markings on its back, and that's a good sign.'

'Good for what?' I asked.

'Good for everything,' he said. 'Luck, the journey, the weather.'

It was May Day, and we were starting out from Gougane on a pilgrimage to the holy well at Crobdearg, near Rathmore in Kerry. Patty had come from across the lake to join us, and Eileen Buckley whose parents live not far from Rathmore, and Mick Riordan, a Kerryman, who like Eileen works at Gougane, were coming too.

The snail certainly made one true prediction, for we had scarcely gone a mile on our course when we were lucky not to kill an old man on the road. 'There wasn't the width of a table between us.' Being stone deaf he didn't hear us coming, and walked into the middle of the road immediately in front of the van. The 'width of a table' grew narrower as the day went on until by the time we reached home it wasn't the width of a plank.

We took the mountainy road from Ballingeary to meet the main Cork to Killarney road at the Half-way House—half-way between Cork and Killarney, half-way between Cork and Bantry, half-way between Macroom and Ballyvourney, and half-way between any other two places that are equidistant from it. It was, of course, necessary to stop there to wet the day, but I was not allowed to put coin on the counter. 'You're earning the hard pound to-day with your driving,' said Patty. 'And I tell you this,' he added, 'the harder the shilling you make, the farther it will go; soft money goes with the air.'

'Where there's been a gathering, there'll be a squandering. Isn't that what they say?' said our hostess.

'The thousands are no good,' said Patty. 'Since ever I wore a shoe I asked no more than would carry me on.'

From the Half-way I drove with a gentle accompaniment of song. Michael's spirits rose higher and higher as we came nearer to his native county. We were constantly meeting friends of his on the road, all of whom had to be greeted, some of whom had to be taken on board for a lift. Whereas there were four in the van when we left Gougane, that number was doubled by the time we reached the county bounds.

But at the Clydagh bridge where we turned north towards Eileen's house our numbers were back to normal. Dan Foley, a friend of Michael's, came from his house to greet us. ''Tis the dreariest May Day I ever saw—a very cold air,' he said. Was it to the City we were going? It was. Then he told us how his mother had been cured after a pilgrimage to Gougane. 'Paralysed she was,' he said, 'and she but a middle-aged woman. She couldn't move a step without help. And 'twas the way on account of that that she couldn't make the journey herself, so said she to a friend: ''Will you go for me and will you make the round for me, and will you pray for me?" she said. "I will," said the friend. So the friend went off to Gougane, and the mother was alone here in the house with a helping girl. And when the time came, the girl put her to bed, for do you see she couldn't move without help. And the girl thought to shut the door when she went out, but it blew open after her. By God, when the mother seen that, she put her legs over the side of the bed and instead of crawling didn't she walk to the door and shut it, and that was between the first and the second rounds at Gougane. And she was all right ever after.'

Leaving Dan Foley, we followed the narrow road a mile or more until we reached Eileen's home, a farmhouse set on the side of the hill overlooking the River Flesk, a fine stream for trout. It was taken for granted that we should all go into the house, and no sooner were we sitting round the open fire than Eileen's sister came in from the next room carrying a trayful of tumblers of whiskey. Conversation flowed, beginning with everyday topics such as turkeys, geese, turf, and spuds, but gradually ranging into wider spheres until it finished up in song. And interspersed with song were step-dances to the accompaniment of 'puss-music,' that is to say a rhythm of sounds, meaningless as bird song, uttered to the tune of a jig or hornpipe. And while the songs and dances were following each other the table was being laid, and soon we were sitting down to a meal with another trayful of glasses handed round. After the meal there were stories and more dances, and then with the addition of a few new passengers to the van we set out for 'the City.'

Why the shrine is called the City it is hard to tell. The remains of a great circular wall suggest that at one time there may have been a fortress there. The Church discountenances the idea that water from the well gives strength to ailing cattle, nevertheless pilgrims flock thither not only to pray but to carry back bottles of the water for their animals. I asked Patty what he thought about it. 'You should never break an old custom,' he said.

We turned up a winding track through mountains. The higher we went the steeper it became, with a surface of loose, slaty stones scarcely concealing large boulders. A number of people on foot or in carts were going the same way. We drove through a pass under the Paps with a small and sullen lake beside us until, reaching the hill whereon the City is built, we left the van and joined the threads of people picking their way up the rocky hill-side. On the bare summit, within and without the mass of broken masonry, suppliants were moving from station to station, kneeling and praying, marking with a pebble the sign of the cross on stones already deeply grooved by centuries of worship. At the entrance was the well, enclosed by its own low wall, a small pool muddied by much disturbance. Men and women of all ages were filling bottles with the water to take home. 'You must let fall three drops into the cow's right nostril and then three into her right ear and then three into her mouth, and you must say a prayer with each and she 'll be strong for the year,' I was told. An old woman with notebook in hand was putting down the names of those who left with her a coin; later she would do a round on their behalf.

I bid the time of day to an old man who was sitting on a rock near by.

'You are a stranger here?' he asked.

'I 'm from Cork,' I told him.

'Do you see that small little field before you?' he said. ''Tis no more than thirty yards each way, and there was a time when you could put every horse and cow in Kerry and Cork into it and there 'd still be room for more. People would drive their cattle here at that time, to be cured, if they had the murrain or another sickness. But I don't think it is the same to-day.'

'Do you know who the saint was that was here?' I asked.

'That is a true puzzle,' he said, 'for the learned men to-day are bad talkers and bad writers with the pen, and bad thinkers, and all the sayings of the old men—and they were brave men, you see, gifted by God, you couldn't better them to-day—all their sayings and doings are scattered and blown like smoke through the country.'

'I was told,' I said, 'that it was a brother of St. Finnbarr was here.'

'I do not think so,' he said. 'You have heard about St. Brigid? I believe it was she was the saint. If you sit down on that stone there beside me, I will tell you about her.'

I sat down.

'You see,' he said, 'she lived in the County of Kildare and she worked with a gentleman and he was very fond of her, and he gave her charge and control over all his business, all his cattle, butter, and milk. And it seems that one day she went over and above the limits in real charity, and when she looked in the vessels there wasn't one drop or sup. Says she, I'll be killed in the evening when the master comes home, and she was in deep grief. But, says she, God is good and that's about it, and with that she said a prayer. When she looked in the vessels again, wasn't each one of them flowing to the top, full to the mouth. So when the master came home everything was all right, and she never let on to him a word about the day's doings. And that woman, I believe, is the woman who built the City for the people. The cattle used to be sick and suffering from sickness of several kinds so she came to that City and built the shrine there.'

'Wasn't it St. Brigid who built the first church in Kildare?' I asked.

'Why, to be sure she did. 'Twas the same gentleman gave her the land. Says she to him one day, "I must be leaving you," she says. "And why so?" says he. "I cannot spend all my life with you," she says. "Well," says he, "if you must, you must, but is there anything I can do for you before you go?" "You have treated me well and given me substantial pay," she said, "but I will ask you one thing. Will you give me the breadth of my shawl in the County of Kildare and I will build a church there?" "Get your shawl and spread it," says he. So she took her shawl and she caught it by the four corners and she shook it as you might give a shake to your handkerchief, and didn't it spread over five square miles. "'Tis yours," says he, "'tis all yours." And that's where she built the church and the convent.'

My fellow pilgrims joined me. They were ready to go home. This time we took a longer road to avoid the boulders. We didn't stop till we reached Ballyvourney.

It was in this neighbourhood, some few years ago, that a circular disk of gold was dug up, about four inches in diameter and ornamented with rings of small chevrons, which by its analogy with a disk found in Trundholm in Denmark seems to have direct connection with sun worship. In September 1902, on Trundholm Island, when some land was being freshly cultivated, the plough turned up an almost complete miniature waggon of bronze on which was carried a model of a horse drawing a bronze disk faced on one side with gold, believed to represent the sun.

The disk from Ballyvourney is but one of many from various parts of Ireland, now in the National Museum in Dublin and elsewhere. Another was found near Ballydehob, a town in County Cork which only a few years ago also produced the world's champion all-in wrestler. After his return from America, bringing with him all the titles and honours of his profession, it was reported in the local press that his entry into his native town was Caesarian. Many gold ornaments found in County Cork were for a time in the collection of my grandfather, Robert Day. I can still remember his excitement after four farmers had called to see him, in 1907. At first sight, he said, 'they seemed like a deputation from some football or sports club, looking for a subscription.' 'I dunno would you be interested in these kind of things,' said the spokesman, producing from one of his pockets a gold fibula and from the other a bronze axe head. 'We have another one of each of the two, west at Coachford, and there's a string of brown beads along with them. 'Twas when digging for a fence that we came on them.'

Though nothing is known for certain as to the purpose of these fibulae, of which a large number have been discovered in Ireland, it is thought that they were used as fastenings for cloaks or other loose garments. The idea may have been brought from Denmark or Sweden, for there was much intercourse between Ireland and Scandinavia from the ninth to the seventh centuries B.C. The beads, which proved to be of amber, probably came from Scandinavia also.

Exquisite necklets of twisted gold ribbon, known as torques; crescent-shaped plates of gold, some eight inches in diameter, burnished and fin'ely chased, known as lunulae, possibly worn as collars or as hair decorations; richly embossed gorgets, bracelets, rings, and other ornaments  have been found in quantity all over Ireland. It has been said that 'though the Irish gold antiquities at present known can only represent a small part of the original wealth of the country in this metal, the amount would probably exceed that of any ancient period in any country, except perhaps the republic of Columbia in South America.' It has been suggested, too, that the main reason for the invasion of Ireland by the Celts was their desire to obtain possession of the gold-fields in County Wicklow, and there is evidence that the Normans at the time of their invasion of the country believed that the Irish kings controlled secret gold-mines. As late as the year 1795 a nugget weighing twenty-two ounces was found in County Wicklow. After passing through various hands, it was presented to King George III who had it converted into a snuff-box.

At Castle Martyr, near Youghal, a labourer when working in a stone quarry let fall his crowbar through a fissure in the rock. Determined not to lose the implement, he widened the crevice and crept through in search of it. Not only did he find the crowbar but there before him he saw lying a human skeleton partly covered with plates of gold. This may well have been the mortal remains of one of the four kings, who, according to tradition, were killed in battle near the site of the quarry. Unfortunately, the finder of the gold disposed of most of it to a jeweller—'rather more than the contents of half a coal box'; but one of the plates, about two inches in length, was allowed to survive, and in due course came into my grandfather's possession. To-day it is in the Dublin museum.

A more recent and equally exciting find, a small gold ornament representing a wren, was made in 1945 during the excavation of a ring-fort at Garryduff, a village about twenty miles to the north-east of Cork. In size the bird is no bigger than the nail of one's little finger, and yet it is of the most elaborate and superb craftsmanship, being built up of several pieces of gold foil and richly ornamented with a filigree of beaded gold wire. The fragments of pottery and bronze found with the bird suggest a date not later than the sixth century, and it is an interesting conjecture that there may be some association, however remote, between it and a custom that still survives. In County Cork and other parts of Ireland, on St. Stephen's Day, 26th December, you will meet groups of boys with blackened faces, in strange attire, carrying a furze or holly bush at the top of which hangs among sundry tawdry accessories the body of an unfortunate wren. And outside your door these little hooligans will sing for your entertainment and their reward:

 ' "The wren, the wren, the king of all birds,
  St. Stephen's Day was caught in the furze,
  And though he is little his family 's great,
  Arise, good sir, and give us a treat.

  Mr. Gibbings is a worthy man
  And to his house we 've brought the wran,
  Up with the kettle and down with the pot,
  Give us our ransom and let us be got.'' '

This custom of hunting the wren is not confined to Ireland. In one form or another it is almost as widespread as the attribute of royalty assigned to the bird. The Latin name *regulus*, the French *roitelet*, the Spanish *reyezuelo*, the Italian *reatino*, as well as German and Scandinavian names, all signify 'king.' The well-known story of the wren concealing itself cn the eagle's back, when by a contest in high flying the birds were electing their sovereign, is common also to all these countries.

There are many legends to account for this yearly sacrifice, some of them religious, some political, and others merely fanciful. Among the latter is the story, from the Isle of Man, of a fairy who by her beauty lured men to the sea and drowned them. Whenever, in self-defence, the men of the island pursued her, she would change into a wren and so evade capture. Eventually they were able to cast a spell which compelled her to take the form of a wren on each St. Stephen's Day, when it became incumbent on every male to hunt her down and destroy her.

For the true explanation of this custom one would probably need to go back to pagan times, a period to which this little gold ornament may well belong. Evidence shows that the Celts regarded the wren as a divine creature, perhaps totemic. The annual sacrifice might therefore be analogous to the Siberian custom of leading a bear through the village, before it was slain, or to a similar ritual with a snake in the Punjab. As Sir James Frazer has suggested, it would be 'a form of communion in which the sacred animal is taken from house to house, that all may enjoy a share of its divine influence.'

In Ireland the wren was at one time known as the 'Druid bird'—the bird that makes a prediction. It was said that if any one understood its chirpings he or she would have a knowledge of the future as foretold by the bird.   From this perhaps comes our expression: 'A little bird told me.'

At Ballyvourney we rested a while in Williams's store, an establishment that seemed to hold everything needful to man or beast.   On our left as we went in were pig troughs, pitch-forks, scythes, coils of wire; on the shelves opposite to the door were sweets for children, purges for cattle, laxatives for humans, dips for sheep, and tonics for laying hens; from the ceiling hung halters for horses' heads, spancels for cows' heels, mudguards for bicycles, hanks of knitting wool, wire bottle brushes, frying-pans, and buckets; on the floor were sacks of grass seed and sacks of flour, cans of creosote, rolls of barbed wire and tins of engine oil.   'There isn't a thing in the world you couldn't get here if you wanted it,' said Patty. On the right of the store behind a counter was what we wanted.   But we didn't stay long, only just enough to set my passengers singing again, this time a variant of *The Green Willow*:

'"All round my hat I wear the green, white and yel-low,
  All round my hat till death comes to me,
  And if anybody asks me why I'm wearing that rib-bon,
  It is for my true love who set old Ireland free."'

A mile to the east of Ballyvourney we met a party of young men on the road, one of them with his coat off, playing 'a score of bowls,' a game whose stronghold is in County Cork, though north of the border, in Armagh, it is also popular. All that is needed is a twenty-eight-ounce iron ball and the open road before you, about four or four and a half miles of it, according to the distance between two convenient pubs. In a big match there would be only two players, one against the other, and the stakes might be £100 or £150 a side; but in a friendly game, with no money involved, there are often two players on each side. The aim and object of the game is to get the bowl to its destination in the least number of throws. The player takes a run and, 'jumping in' to the line, swings his arm a complete circle before letting the bowl go in an under-arm throw. 'And the roar that goes up when a good bowl is thrown! "He's lit the road!"' meaning that he has knocked sparks out of the stones. A good player can 'loft' the bowl as much as seventy yards before it touches the ground, and after that it might run for nearly a quarter of a mile, gathering speed with the spin on it. 'You should see it tear along the road with a trail of dust after it, like a bullet, and every one lepping in the air and shouting and flaking the road with their ash-plants.' Whoever has thrown the 'hind bowl' throws again, and so it goes on until either player gets a full throw ahead of his opponent or one of them has reached the final mark.

Legally speaking the game is illegal, and to-day fines are not so nominal as they were—the cost of living has gone up; but still the game flourishes and matches are advertised regularly in the local press. 'After all, what danger is it to the public with a man well ahead to warn the traffic? Isn't it far less dangerous than the motors that are travelling the roads, killing and destroying in every direction?'

No one minds an officer doing his duty and no one minds an occasional small fine, but when a guardian of the law loses all sense something has to be done. 'There was a policeman and he was for ever fining the boys; every evening he'd be out taking away their bowls and getting convictions. So one day they went along to the forge on the hill, and they reddened a bowl in the smith's fire, and when they got word that the policeman was coming along they carried the bowl out on a shovel and sent it rolling down the hill. When the police-man seen it coming, he stopped it under his boot and he picked it up to put it in his pocket. Well, if he was quick to pick it up, he was quicker to drop it. I tell you, 'twas some time before he interfered again.'

As is usual, the game that evening was held up while we passed through. The man ahead, 'showing the road,' had signalled our approach. Showing the road to the players is a very important part of the play. There are places where the bowl will run straight, others where the camber can be made to help in manœuvring a curve or which, if not watched, may throw the bowl from its course. The man ahead indicates the best spot at which to aim.

By the time we had passed the Half-way House the sun had set, and as often happens after dusk the car seemed to be running particularly well. I thought of 'Chester Billy' of the old coaching days. 'Do you mean to say you don't know the reason why the horses go faster after dark? Why, it's because you 've 'ad your dinner!'

'Did ye have a good day?' asked Connie Cronin when we reached Gougane.

'A great day,' said Patty.

'And he drove ye well?'

'Yerra,' said Patty, 'he could drive through the eye of a snail.'

CHAPTER ELEVEN

THE STORY GOES that to Derranaburka, 'the Wood of the Spancel,' a few miles east of Gougane, a woman went one evening to milk her cow. There was a nice bit of grass between the trees, and she would often drive the cow over there to graze for a few days. And this night she carried with her a spancel for the animal's hind legs, for it was inclined to be crabbity when being milked. But when the woman got to the wood there wasn't a sign of the cow. She looked everywhere among the oak-trees, and in places they were very thick, but no sign at all. And just when she thought she 'd lost the animal for ever she saw at the foot of a tree a firkin and it was full of gold. It was, of course, too heavy for her to carry, so with the spancel she had in her hand she tied it to the tree and hurried back to Gougane for help. And all the boys went with her to help her. But when they got into the wood they found a spancel round every tree, the cow grazing where she 'd been left in the morning, and not a sign of the firkin.

To-day nothing remains of the wood but gnarled roots, and those living in the neighbourhood will not discuss the story. ''Twould bring too many people digging, and there's been enough trouble already with people disturbing the old places.'

I asked old Corney Donnelan, the story-teller who lives near the Kerry border, if he could explain it to me. 'There is always something in the way of you getting the gold,' he said slowly. 'It may be an animal of some kind, maybe a dog or a pig that is in charge of it, that will play tricks on you and put you in the wrong way. I was in a farm one time,' he went on, 'and I came home one evening, and in the night I dreamed that I went to work with the horse in the field the day after and there was a big box of gold in the field, deep in the ground, and I dreamed that the horse would go down in it. Sure enough, in the morning, in the second ridge of the field, didn't the horse's leg go down, down deep into the ground. And I remembered then what went through my mind in the night and I thought of the dream and I thought of the gold and I was near stunned on the spot. The horse pulled herself out of the hole and she wasn't hurt at all. So I shovelled and I shovelled till I met stones, and when I pulled out the stones the floor under them was even and smooth and hard. And while I was doing that, a small little man walked up to me and says he: "Is it mad you are getting or what?" And I said: "I'm not mad yet." And he had a yellow dog with him, and the dog made a drive at the horse and frightened her. So I put down the shovel while I went to quieten the horse, and when I went back to the hole it was all filled in and there was no more than a stick in the ground where I'd left the shovel, and there was no sign of the little man or the dog.'

'Did you try again?' I asked him.

'I did not,' he said, 'but I tell you this, that every time since in my natural life that I walk across that field I hear it hollow under my feet. I think,' he added, 'that the night is the best time to go after the gold, and you 'd want to take with you the holy water and all that class of thing to help you.'

Stories of buried treasure often have their origin in periods of war and unrest. There must be many people living in Europe to-day who are seeking valuables which were buried at the threat of invasion. Those who hid the treasures may have died or been killed before they could recover what they had concealed. A few last words to a relative or friend— the beginning of a legend—may be the only clue.

But reverting to the past, it was no doubt due to continuous disappointment and frustration on the part of those who sought for easy reward that there grew up, not only in Ireland but in many other countries, the idea that buried treasure comes under the special care of supernatural beings. In Morocco it is believed that hidden wealth is always guarded by *jinn* who appear in many disguises, the favourite role being that of a cat. Nobody in Morocco would dare to hit a cat after dark—a cat in that country has seven lives, and to kill one would be as bad as to kill seven men. In 1950 a real cat seen by a guide on the Matterhorn was mistaken by him for the ghost cat that guards treasure hidden in the lake at the foot of the mountain. Dr. Westermarck tells of two Berbers and an Arab who sought for treasure among ruins not far from Marrakesh. After they had begun their excavations a big snake came out of the ground and opened its mouth at them but, as they took no notice of its threats, it went away. They continued with the digging until they came upon two boxes, fastened together with rings. No sooner had these been brought to light than a black girl appeared and, putting a foot on one of the boxes, said to the diggers: 'Are you not ashamed to take our money? Go away or I will throw you away.' The Arab who was doing the digging replied that he would go but, before the others had had time to speak, one of them was flung to a considerable distance from where they had been working, while the other was hurled even further, and so violently that he died. When the Arab, who had escaped unhurt, returned to the site he found the hole filled in. It is not so long ago that the Borderers of England and Scotland, when burying money or goods, committed them with incantations to the care of 'that faithful ally of the household,' the Brownie, sprinkling the treasure with the blood of a slaughtered animal or perhaps burying the animal with it.

Many people to-day are inclined to smile at stories of 'crocks of gold,' often attributing to them a mere symbolic significance, but there may well be more truth in these tales than is at first imagined. There was a tradition among the people of Walton-le-Dale in Lancashire that if you stood on a certain hill and looked northwards up the valley of the Ribble, 'you would gaze over the greatest treasure that England had ever seen.' This proved to be true when, after nearly a thousand years, the treasure was brought to light in 1840. In an almost perished leaden case within a crumbling wooden box lay ingots of silver, armlets, rings, and chains, and along with them some ten thousand silver coins, in all 'sufficient to cover the floor of one of the sitting-rooms in Cuerdale Hall' near by. The bulk of the coins was Danish, but nearly a thousand of them were of the reign of King Alfred, as the inscription AEL-FRE-DREX clearly shows. Others were of French origin. It was the treasure chest of the Danes who, about the year 911, after raiding Mercia, were followed by the English and defeated. Unable  to cross the Ribble in their retreat, they had buried their treasure near by, where eventually it was discovered by men working on the bank of the river. The Danes being out-flanked by the English in a bend of that river had been slain to a man; it was the rearguard, coming up later, who, knowing that their wealth had been concealed but not knowing where to look for it, had by their actions or perhaps words given rise to the legend. So strongly had this tradition persisted through the centuries that one night about the year 1580 two men, Sir Edward Kelley and a friend of his, Paul Waring, went to the churchyard of Walton-le-Dale and dug up the corpse of a reputed miser, endeavouring by incantations to learn from him the whereabouts of the hoard. The fact that the hoard was not discovered until after another two hundred and fifty years had passed suggests that either Sir Edward and his friend had exhumed the wrong man or that there was a technical flaw in their spells.

Another instance comes from Scotland where, near the Fifeshire coast, there was the tradition that a tumulus known as Norrie's Law held a 'siller hoard that was whumlet in to the deep lair o' the warrior-chieftain Tam o' Norrie, slain in weir'—Tam in all probability being Thomas of Norway, a Norse pirate who settled on that coast during the ninth century. About the year 1819, a tinker when 'digging for sand' in the tumulus found and disposed of about four hundred ounces of silver before being apprehended. The owner of the land then continued with the excavations and unearthed a quantity of silver brooches, torques, plates, and coins.

Towards the end of the seventeenth century, when the Lord Bishop of Derry was dining with a friend of his at Ballyshannon in County Kildare, 'there came in an Irish Harper and sang an old song to his harp.' The song being in Irish nobody at table understood his words, but a herdsman was called in to interpret for them. The song told, he said, that in a certain place there lay buried a man of gigantic stature, and that over his breast and back were plates of pure gold and on his fingers rings of gold 'so large than an ordinary man might creep through them.' Some of the guests went in search next day and found two pieces of gold, which seemed to bear out the harper's words; unfortunately they also found evidence that the grave had been tampered with at an earlier date, and there was no sign of either the giant or his rings.

It was when Pat Brendan came to stay at Gougane that I heard of Glaunagalt, 'the Valley of the Lunatics,' in County Kerry. 'We must go there one day,' he said. Then he told me that if any lunatic in Ireland is left to himself he will find his way to that valley, and if he drinks of the well there he will be cured.

'Which of us needs a drop?' I asked him.

'Prevention is better than cure,' he said.

So off we went, with turbulent streams left and right of the road, over the hills to Killarney, and then through rich pasture land to Tralee and thence westwards, with the sea on our right and the Slieve Mish mountains piling high on our left. Many a wanderer on those hills has seen a man standing on the top of a high crag with a large black dog beside him; but no one knows who he is, for when approached he disappears. Only once has his voice been heard. A farmer crossing the hills, alone, thought to take a pinch of snuff. He was about to put the snuff-box back in his pocket when he heard a voice. 'Hold on a while, take your time!' it said to him. He looked around but could see no one. Again he was going to put the box away when the voice said to him: 'Hold on, hold on! I am near you.' Not knowing what to do, the owner of the snuff-box shook a pinch of it into the palm of his hand and held it out. Judge of his feelings when he felt fingers that he could not see taking the snuff and, a moment later, heard a sneeze. 'The Lord

between us and all harm!' he ejaculated, terrified.   'Amen,'
said the voice.

If ever a man could find release from the distortions of a
troubled spirit, it should be in Glaunagalt.   There in that
maternal valley old wounds should heal and the scars of the
mind vanish.   On either side the breasts of the hills slope
gently downwards to a flower-margined stream whose notes

mingle with bird song in the copses. There is not a harsh line in all the contours. Hedges trace the boundaries of fields as though a net had been thrown across the land.

As Pat and I walked down the lane into the valley, an elderly farmer came from a nearby field and greeted us. Was it the spring we were looking for? He could show it to us. He 'd come along.

Pat offered him a fill of his pipe.

No, he didn't smoke and he didn't drink. 'That 's one gift I have anyway,' he said. 'And all my relatives are smokers and drunkards. I didn't even drink when I was in America. Maybe 'twas because I hadn't much English when I crossed over—I could understand it, d'ye see, but I couldn't make company with it. I was only a young fellow at the time. I came back after four years. Damn glad I was, too, to be back. 'Tis happier at home, and healthier too. Isn't it a terror the number of sicknesses is in the world, a hundred and sixty-nine of them, and every one of them watching you and waiting for a chance to get a grip on you. Sure, how can a man escape? If it wasn't for them you'd live for ever.'

I inquired if there had been many cures in the valley.

'There 's been many,' he said, 'and I 'm telling you no lie. There was a girl brought here a few years back. Raving mad she was, fighting and struggling. She threw herself down on the road at this very corner, and she cut her head on a stone and she bleeded a fright of blood. But they got her to the stream and after she 'd taken a drink from it she went away quiet and sensible as the rest of us.'

While we talked I noticed that he was watching us carefully, eyeing each of us in turn. Then having made up his mind, apparently, which of the two was afflicted, he whispered to me: 'Is he mad?'

'I don't think he's even been in love,' I said.

'He must be mad,' said our guide.

Then as Pat knelt beside the stream and cupped the water to his lips with his hands, the old man disappeared into a thicket. He reappeared a few minutes later with an armful of watercress. 'Take this with you,' he said, 'and eat it. 'Tis good for the brain.' We thought no more of his remark at the time than of similar advice often given about the eating of fish; but a few weeks later, reading in an old herbal, I came across the fact that among the Greeks watercress was highly esteemed as a curative for disorders of the brain, so much so that there was a saying common among them: 'Go eat cress,' applied to those whose wits were thought to be deficient.

That is not the only connection between Ireland and Greece. There is, for instance, an amazing similarity between some of the legends. How this has come about is not certain. It may be that Phoenician traders, hearing these stories in the Aegean, repeated them when they reached Ireland; or if, as old traditions suggest, the early inhabitants of Ireland were of oriental origin, the stories may have had a common birthplace with those in Greece. A number of the incidents related by Homer in the Iliad bear a close resemblance to tales by oriental writers, or to myths current in the Indian Archipelago. One of the most striking parallels is the story of the Irish king who had ears of immoderate length and the Greek story of Midas who suffered under a like affliction. In the Irish version, the king wishing to conceal the deformity ordained that each barber who trimmed his hair should be put to death immediately after the operation. Then one day the lot fell on a young man, the only son of a widow. Distraught with grief, she appealed to the king and by her lamentations persuaded him to spare her son's life.

But there was one condition attached to this clemency: the young man must give his oath that he would not reveal a secret which in the performance of his duty he might discover. Needless to say the terms were accepted, and gladly. But as time went on the knowledge that the youth had gained preyed on his mind. The sight of the ears haunted his dreams at night and was ever in his mind during the day. He longed to share the secret with another. Eventually the obsession made him ill; he grew weaker and weaker, and it was thought that he would die. Then his friends consulted a Druid, and the Druid divined the cause. 'There is a secret,' he said to the sufferer, 'that lies heavy on your mind. You must go to a place where four roads meet, and there you must whisper your secret to the ground.' The youth did as he was told. He went to a place where four highways met, he dug a hole, and into the opened earth he whispered the cause of his sorrow. Immediately he was cured: his obsession left him. But not long afterwards the king's harper, needing some timber to repair his harp, chose a willow-tree from beside where the secret had been buried. Behold, when the harp was mended it would sound only one strain: 'Two ears of a horse hath the king.' In the Greek version Midas, King of Phrygia, having angered Apollo by giving judgment against him in a musical contest, had a pair of ass's ears bestowed upon his person by the offended deity. Midas, anxious to conceal the deformity, swore his barber to secrecy. And, again, the barber goes forth and digs a hole and whispers into it: 'King Midas has ass's ears.' Before long there grew above the hidden secret a cluster of reeds, and as the wind played through them they seemed to say: 'Midas has ass's ears.'

Herodotus, the Greek historian, narrates that whilst the army of King Darius was subduing Thrace, seven Persian noblemen, ambassadors of Darius, were entertained by King Amyntas of Macedon in his palace. Towards the end of the banquet the Persians, replete with food and wine, called on their host to bring in his wives and his sisters. This suggestion, being contrary to all the laws of etiquette and hospitality of that country, infuriated Alexander, the king's son. He gave instructions that a number of young men were to be dressed as women but with poniards hidden in their clothes. Thus disguised they entered the hall and, when occasion arose, fell on the Persian nobles and slew them. An almost identical story is told in Ireland as having occurred in County Meath when Maolseachluin brought about the destruction of Turgesius and his Danes by a similar stratagem.

In the story of 'Dermat O'Dyna, of the Bright Face, the favourite of maidens,' we have an Irish version of the legend of Adonis. Both are cautioned against hunting the wild boar, both are killed by that same animal, and in both narratives the boar is presented to us as a rational being who has been metamorphosed for the express purpose of destroying the hunter.

Danae locked in her tower yet giving birth to Perseus has her counterpart in the daughter of Balor who, in spite of similar restraints, went two better and produced three sons at one birth. In each case the grandfather is killed by the mother's avenging offspring.

CHAPTER TWELVE

AT FIVE O'CLOCK on a morning early in June, Jer Riordan, Michael Kelly, Timmy Leary, and Dan Borlin, with four dogs, were away on the mountains, rounding up the sheep that with their lambs were stravaging about on that great battlement of hills which guards the northern side of Gougane Barra lake.

It was shearing time, and if all the sheep on that side of the valley were to be dealt with before dark they 'd have to be down in the pen early. It was no trouble to Jer to be on the high ridges at that hour, for he has no more spare flesh on him than a hairpin, and there 's never been one hour in the twenty-four when he hasn't had one eye open. It was no trouble to Timmy Leary, either, for he is as lean as a squirrel and as active. After nine years planting conifers on inaccessible slopes, the grazing ground of a sheep is no more to him than a croquet lawn to another. Michael Kelly, with all the eagerness of youth, is as good as the best, and Dan Borlin, who had come seven miles over the mountain the night before for the fun of it, is better than the best.   Dan is a giant: it is nothing to him to carry a hundredweight sack of cement under each arm as if they were kittens.   It is nothing to him to run down a sheep on the mountains at the end of the day, when his two dogs are only capable of limping home.   He wears his cap with the peak to the back of his head, his face might have been dipped in a tan barrel, his eyes are dazzling blue, and the strength in his long lean limbs would frighten you.

'I wouldn't like to get a clout from his fist,' I said to Jer.

'A clout?' said Jer.   'He wouldn't hit a fly.'

By ten o'clock in the morning all the sheep—ewes, wethers, rams, and lambs—had been safely gathered, and the boys came home for breakfast.   But in less than an hour they were back again at the pens and had begun shearing.   And now they were joined by Dan Borlin's brother Con, and Jer Riordan's brother Mick, and Jackie Buckley who had taken a day off from the roads.

The seven shearers were strung out along the narrow path beside the sheepfold, each with an animal held between his knees while he worked.   Above them, holly- and rowan-trees spreading from rents in huge boulders gave shade from the morning sun.   To the north, a half-acre of meadow sloped down to a strip of bog, rich in royal fern, that bounded the head of the lake.   The lake itself, fringed with tall reeds and rushes, glistened with water-lilies.   The sorrel-tinted buds of the pondweed promised a change of raiment in the weeks to come.   And over all, sheer from the water's edge, rose rugged bastions of purple rock, interspersed with the bright green of young conifers and the darker shades of oak and birch.

As each man gave the last snick of the shears to a fleece, he took the animal by the horns and held it while Breda, ten-year-old daughter of the house, ran forward with a tin of blue stain, and with a stick marked two broad bands across the creature's shoulders. Then it was set free to join its naked fellows on the hill-side.

Meanwhile, Connie Gougane was making a note of each animal as it passed through the shearers' hands. 'Is it wet or dry?' he would ask, meaning was it a ewe still feeding her lamb, or one who had not had a lamb—who had 'missed,' or maybe lost her lamb through foxes. Or it might be a yearling wether or a ram. There was one big ram, a three-year-old—you could tell by the number of twists in his horns—but he didn't belong. He had come gallivanting over the mountains, and had a red raw lump on the top of his head, behind his horns, from butting other rams.

'Isn't it late in the season for fighting?' I asked.

'It's late enough all right,' said Connie, 'but there was a weakness in the rams this year and many of the ewes missed. Maybe 'twas that was the reason.'

And now we could see two girls from the house bringing refreshment for the workers. Nell came first, her fair hair shining in the sunlight, her pink-flowered frock matching the plumes of London Pride that clothed every rock. After her strode Mary, with six bottles of hot tea suspended in thick woollen stockings from her shoulders. When they came to the stepping-stones across the river Nell picked her way with care, but Mary, swinging the bottles around her head, jumped from stone to stone with the agility of a sheep just released from the shearers.

Now was the time for gossip and chat, each man sitting on the ground with a bottle of tea before him and a bunch of sandwiches in his fist.

'Pat Downey got a great price for his cattle at Bantry,' said Michael.

'How did he manage it at all?' asked Jer.

''Twas Shaun Flavin helped him,' said Michael. When Pat drove the cattle in, he left them on the square, as if he didn't give a damn about them. He just walked off and began talking with Dan Duggan, from west of Ardnagashel.'

'They say Dan's son is doing wonders in London.'

'Ah, them Duggans is full of brains. Sure, wasn't Mick the grandest doctor in the world? If he never did anything for you, you'd be satisfied. And there's young Dan now, and he at the top of the tree in London without as much as opening a book.'

'What was Shaun doing at Bantry?'

'Helping Pat Downey; amn't I telling you?'

'But he wouldn't be known in Bantry.'

'Isn't that the fun? Sure he walks about for a bit, and then he comes up and has a look at Pat's cattle. "Who's selling?" says he. "The fellow west in the grey hat," says someone. With that there was a shout for Pat Downey, and Pat comes over, slowly, no hurry at all. "How much do you want?" says Shaun, pretending he'd never seen him before. "Eighteen a head," says Pat. "I'll give you sixteen," says Shaun. Pat turns his back on him. "Don't be wasting my time," he says. "Sixteen ten," says Shaun in a loud voice. Pat paid no attention. And there was a bunch of fellows listening, and among them was Tim Lehane. Tim's no good with cattle—he's as good a judge of a horse as there is in Kerry, but he's no good with the cattle. So he waits, do you see, till he thinks he's heard the value from another fellow. "Sixteen fifteen," says Shaun. "I'd as soon sell them to you for nothing," says Pat. "Seventeen," says Shaun. "Look at them," says Pat, "eighteen is the price." "Seventeen ten," says Shaun, lifting his hand to strike the bargain. Pat walked away. "I dunno will I give it," says Shaun and off he walks too.'

It is an understood thing at fairs in Ireland that a third party will never cut in while bargaining is going on; but he is perfectly free to do so when either of the men walks away.

'And then along comes Tim Lehane,' continued Michael. 'He 'd been listening all the time. "Whisper," says he to Pat, "will you take seventeen fifteen a head?" Pat lifted his hat and scratched his poll. "I 'm giving them to you for it," he says.'

'And what would they be worth?' asked Jer.

'About sixteen five,' said Michael.

Work on the sheep began again, and during the afternoon the girls came back with more tea. By half-past seven the two hundred and thirty-nine sheep had been shorn, and already many of them were gleaming as white dots on the higher ledges of the mountain. But the wool had to be packed and brought home. It was ten o'clock before the shearers sat down to their supper.

By six o'clock next morning the same men had their breakfast taken and were climbing the mountain to the south to gather for another day's shearing. One could see them striding through the heather and ling, and making their way through the fern and bog myrtle, stepping lightly among the tangled rushes and tussocks of sphagnum moss. From the high ridges they could look down on Bantry Bay to the south-west, island-studded like a miniature Aegean. To the north they could see the Kerry hills—Mangerton of the Red Hair flanked by the swelling Paps of Dana and the cone of Carrantuohill. There is plenty in those mountains to think about, if one has a mind for it: the hidden lakes that hold big trout, the eagles that once nested there, the red deer and the

fairies that still people the hillsides.   But instead, it was the
sheep on their own hills that called for the men's attention.
One hundred and fifty-six they brought down, and these were
shorn by four o'clock in the afternoon.   Again the men
climbed upwards to bring back another eighty-six from a yet
more distant range.   In the evening light, from across the
valley I could see a molten stream of milk-white fleeces
flowing down the hill-side, with golden dogs leaping and
barking and men in bright ganseys shouting and running.
Darkness was falling before the last bared creature looked
through the open door of the pen, hesitated a moment, then
with a leap across the track bounded forward to join its
fellows, many of them already far away, looking like mere
tufts of cotton grass among the time-stained rocks.

CHAPTER THIRTEEN

ONE WET NIGHT in the kitchen at Gougane, Joan was kneading dough at one end of the table, Connie was slicing rashers at the other end, and the two children, Breda and Margaret, were playing a card game in between. Con Borlin and myself were sitting by the fire.

'Wouldn't you tell us a story, Con?' said Connie.

'I couldn't,' said Con.

'Why not?'

'Sure, you know them all.'

'We do not.'

'Tell us about the king's son,' said Breda.

'You know it already,' said Con.

'I never heard it,' I said.

'You haven't?'

'Never in my life.'

'Go on, Con,' said Connie, ''tis years since I heard it.'

Con paused a few moments to think. 'Well,' he said, ''tis the way there was a king and he had a son, an only son. 'Twas the only son he ever had and he was a fine lad. He was as tall as a tree and as strong as an engine, and he used to be playing hand-ball of an evening up agin the castle walls on the outside. And one evening an old man on a white horse rides up to him and says he: "I 'll play you now and I 'll beat you," he says. "You 'll play me but you won't beat me," says the king's son. Man, he was powerful strong: how could an old man of eighty years beat the likes of him? Maybe he was more than eighty, I couldn't tell you anyway. "I 'll tell you what it is," said the old man, "I 'll play you three times, one game every evening, and if I beats you once you must follow

me, for I 'll take you with me." So they played the first
time and the king's son won, and they played the second time
and the king's son won, and they played the third time, and
'twas a soft afternoon with a bit of a mist spreading over the
land, and didn't the old man win. So the old man says to the
king's son: "You 'll come home with me now," he says.
"I like you greatly," he says. "You 'll be very handy to
me," he says. So up on the back of the white horse the two
of them gets and away they went, flying through the sky, till
at long last they gets to Tir na n-Og. And the old man put the
king's son to bed. "Have a good sleep now," he says,
"for there 's a hard day's work before you in the morning."

'So the king's son had a good sleep and he woke up at dawn
and the old man was awake too, so the two of them got up
and the old man says to him: "Now," says he, "my great-
grandmother lost a bodkin years and years ago and 'tis out in
that heap of manure it is, and if you don't find it for me by
the fall of night I 'll cut the head off of you and eat you."
So with that he gave the lad a dung-fork and he told him try
for the needle. Well, the king's son dug the manure all
day. I couldn't tell you all the trouble he took, parting the
straws with his fingers, and not a sign of the bodkin did he
see. "I 'll be killed, surely," says he in the evening, so he
sat down on a stone and began to cry. And all of a sudden
who did he see standing over him but the old man's daughter
—the grandest lady ever a man saw—and she with the bodkin
in her hand. "Here it is," said she. "Show it to the
father," she said, "but don't let it out of your hand. Don't
give it to him at all," she said. "That needle will be handy
to you yet. 'Twill be useful to you hereafter."

'So then the old man comes along. "Have you found the
bodkin?" says he. "I have," says the king's son, and he
shows it to him, but he doesn't give it out of his hand.

"Good enough," says the old man. "Go to sleep now, for there 's another hard day before you, a harder day than this one," he said. So the king's son went to bed—I dunno did they give him any supper—and he had a good sleep, for he was tired after all the rooting about in the manure. And in the morning he woke up and the old man says to him: "Here 's a gun," he says, "go out and shoot some birds and build a bridge of feathers across that stream below you there to the east." So the king's son went out and he fired and he fired and he couldn't hit one bird. He fired all day without as much as touching a bird, because 'twas a kind of an enchanted gun that he had, d' ye see. By the end of the day he was wore out. "I 'll be killed, surely," said he, and he sat down and began to cry. And along comes the old man's daughter. "I 'll build the bridge for you," she said, and in about twenty minutes wasn't there a bridge of feathers standing across the stream—no bother to her at all.

'So then she comes up to him and says she: "There 'll be a job for you to-morrow and it 's one you 'll never do. He 'll have the head off of you, surely." So at about two o'clock in the night, when all the rest of them was in bed, the king's son and the old man's daughter went down to the stable, and there was two horses in the stable, the one was black and the other was white. So the king's son and the daughter—she was lovely all right—got up on the back of the black horse, and away they struck over the hills. Faith, in the morning when the old man saw what they were after doing, he gets up on the white horse and chases them. And the white horse was faster by half, I tell you he 'd gain a mile in every two on the black one. So when the old man's daughter, sitting up behind the king's son, seen her father coming after them like the wind: "Have you got the bodkin?" says she. "I have," he says. "Throw it over your shoulder," says she. And with that, in twenty seconds wasn't there a thorn wood grown up behind them, three hundred acres of it. So away they went again. But the white horse was too fast for them, and he came round the thorn wood and all of a sudden he was close up on them. "We can't escape him at all," says the king's son. "He's too fast for us altogether." "Is there a drop of moisture in the horse's ear?" said the young girl. "There is," said the king's son. "Take it," she said, "and throw it over your shoulder"—'twas a little drop of moistness, maybe a drop of sweat or the like. So he did as she told him, and next minute wasn't there a lake between them and the old man on the white horse. A lake? 'Twas a whole string of lakes was there, the same as east at Inchigeelah. After that the old man gave up the hunt and went home—"They're too good for me," he said. So the king's son took the daughter back to the palace, and three days and three nights of a marriage feast they had. And 'twas no time at all before the king died, so the king's son took over from his father and the old man's daughter was queen in the palace ever after.'

CHAPTER FOURTEEN

T HE TROUBLE IN IRELAND is not the getting to a place but the getting from it. It would seem that all roads lead to your destination. 'Can you tell me where this road takes me?' asked a friend of mine in County Clare. 'Begor, ma'am, it will take you to anywhere in the world you want to go,' was the reply. The trouble lies in getting away after you have arrived. I once dropped in on a stranger for a cup of tea and I stayed with him for a fortnight. In 1944 I went to Gougane Barra for a fortnight and I stayed there seven months. Five years later I went there in the spring for another fortnight, and stayed there for most of the summer. What with the lake and the island and the mountains and the Cronins I seemed to get anchored.

But now and again I would put my foot on the accelerator and force the van downhill. It was one of these times, a Sunday morning, that I drove through the Pass of Keimaneigh, with its precipitous walls and overhanging cliffs festooned with ivy, and its steep slopes covered with fern and brambles, with foxgloves bursting through and honeysuckle clambering over, and everywhere birch leaves tremulous in the light airs. Keim-an-eigh means 'the Pass of the Deer,' for in the old days the wild deer would move through that narrow defile from one feeding-ground to another in the valleys of the Lee and the Ouvane. Then there was only a track bearing the impress of hoofs: to-day there is a road with all too many trails of tyres.

A few miles from Glengariff I gave a lift to a woman on her way to Mass.

'Four miles there and four miles back every Sunday, on our feet if we don't get a lift,' she said. 'Isn't it a hard road to travel, with purgatory at the end? But,' she added, wrapping her cloak about her knees, 'is the Almighty going to have an empty heaven with only His few saints around Him? Sure, He 'll have to forgive some of us.'

She was one of the old-fashioned folk who still wear the big West-Cork cloaks with hoods, once the pride of every woman, young or old, and handed down from generation to generation as heirlooms. Now, except in a few towns and country districts, they are rarely seen. They always remind me of the faldetta worn by women in Malta, and I have noticed, in Macroom and Kinsale as in Floriana and Valetta, the same gesture of gathering the folds together across the lower part of the face on the approach of a stranger. In Ireland I think it means modesty; in Malta I am sure it means provocation.

As I stopped to put my passenger down outside the chapel,

she thanked me, adding: 'Now I must give you the price of a pint.'

'Ah, no,' I said, '"twas nothing.'

'Oh then, you must have it,' she said, trying to put a coin into my hand.

'No,' I said, 'I couldn't take it at all.'

'But a pint would put pluck in you on the road,' she said.

'Say a prayer for me instead,' I told her.

'Wisha, may the Lord increase you!' she said, and with that she went into the chapel.

My course from Glengariff took me along the north shore of Bantry Bay, as far as Adrigole: ten miles of winding snake-track road through a tortured rocky hill-side. The day being fine, I stopped not once but many times. At Derryconnery I made a drawing of the Sugarloaf Mountain standing in its pride high above the little cultivated patches that speckle the countryside. In these parts a few short ridges of spuds will make a garden, one donkey-load of hay may be the yield of a boulder-studded 'meadow.' At Lough Avaul I watched pied wagtails running on the water-lily leaves, gathering an insect here and there close to the water, or flitting and hovering to catch one a few feet above the surface. One of them alighted on an almost upright bulrush. The rush bent under the weight until its plumed head touched the water. Then the bird took flight and, like a bow-string released, the reed sprang straight again. There was a young moorhen there, too, swimming and diving among the lilies. It was shy of my presence and when coming to the surface would take cover behind one of the broad leaves, whose edge it would shoulder upwards, as though lifted by the wind, until the bird made sure that I had come no closer. And on the far side of the lake I could see a dabchick trying to teach her three fluffy, brownish-black youngsters to dive. Swimming up close to them she would herself dive, reappearing a short distance away with weed in her beak. Immediately the youngsters would rush towards her but, just as they came close, she would dive again, taking the weed with her. The juveniles were not to be tempted. Eventually, tired no doubt of their parent's contrariness, they swam away leaving the mother to continue her activities alone. This she did for a while, as if driven by some instinct. Then she too disappeared among the rushes.

In the afternoon I found myself acting as guide to three girls who had asked me where Biddy the fortune-teller lived. It happened to be less than a mile to her cottage, up a narrow road, but we hadn't gone half that distance when we met the old lady sitting on a low bank beside the lane. She was a small woman, past seventy years of age. A bright handkerchief about her head matched the red of her wrinkled face and the blue of her eyes; otherwise she was dressed in black except for a dingy apron that partly concealed the patches on her voluminous skirt. She and I had met before, but the girls were as much strangers to her as they were to me.

'Will you cut the cards for the ladies?' I asked.

'I will then, and for you too,' she said.

'Where will you do it?' I inquired, expecting to be taken to her cottage.

'We'll do it here on the bank,' she said. As she spoke she lifted her apron and from a deep pocket in her skirt pulled out a pack of cards wrapped in an old and discoloured piece of flannel.

'There's two of you is hearts and that one, the foxy one, and himself is diamonds,' she said, addressing the four of us. Then, speaking to one of the girls: 'Here, take the cards now and cut them into three halves. What's your name?' she asked.

'Eileen,' said the girl.

'Split them now, Eileen,' said Biddy, 'and turn them over with their faces up into the sun. Isn't it grand weather? God be praised, the turf will soon be saved and the hay in. Oh, but isn't there a grand life before you,' she said as she looked at Eileen's cards. 'There's yourself there, the queen of hearts, with the king alongside of you and the ten of diamonds beside the two of ye. God Almighty, how did ye cut it?' It was no great surprise to me to see this particular sequence. I knew that Biddy liked duplicates in her pack.

She took one of the three packs of cards and, going through it, kept up a running commentary.

'There's two rings for you, Eileen,' she said, pointing to the two of diamonds. 'How many have you got on your finger? Only the one! Well, there's another waiting, and you can have it whenever you like. Sure, you could have been married years ago. Look at that club man, now, the knave—you did well to avoid him. He was after you, wasn't he? Aha, don't I know! And why wouldn't he be? Sure, a girl like you could march at the head of a regiment.'

She continued with the cards, warning and advising, and when she had finished with Eileen she made similar prophecies for the other girls. There were club gentlemen breaking their hearts for them, and hearts gentlemen 'making over' money to them, and there were happy homes and immensely large families for all three. Then it came to my turn.

'Tell me,' she whispered, 'which of the three are ye after?'

'I can't decide,' I told her.

'And why wouldn't you have all three?' she asked.

'They mightn't like it,' I said.

'Oh, be damned to you but you 're doing fine with them. Isn't it here in the cards?' Then came predictions of ever-increasing wealth and of a triple family that would more than keep pace with the wealth. We parted with a promise from her of a turkey for the first child.

Unfortunately the girls had been brought up in conservative homes and seemed disinclined to settle down à quatre, so I continued alone on my journey to Adrigole. There I turned inland and followed the road that wound along one side of a vast arena whose upper tiers were pale in a silver haze. A white cottage, lonesome, shone bravely from the hill-side.

The sun was already low when I backed the car into the mouth of a lane and settled down for the night. As twilight crept into the valley, two barefoot children passed me, driving five black heifers before them. They seemed frightened when I spoke to them and hurried on. Not so a man who appeared a little later. He was more anxious for my safety.

'Wouldn't you be afraid to be sleeping out here?' he asked. Well, no, he didn't believe in fairies, but all the same there are things you couldn't believe that you 'd have to believe. He sat down on the stone wall and took a cut of tobacco from the bit of plug I offered him.

'Do you see that sharp corner there behind where you 're after passing?' he asked.

'I do,' I said.

'Well,' he said, 'there was a woman died. She lived about a mile to the west where you 'll be travelling in the morning. And they were taking her down to the grave-yard, and didn't the wheel of the hearse drive into the ditch and the horses took fright and the coffin was thrown out on the road and broke open. 'Twas before they made the Healy pass, a few years back, and the road was very bad.

Out in the road the coffin was thrown and, I suppose 'twas with the shake of it, the woman inside came back to life. So they took her home with them, and she told them stories of heaven and hell and purgatory, and she said that the lowest down in hell was the bailiffs. Faith, she went on telling the stories till the priest came in and stopped her. And she lived for three years after, and then she died again. And this time when they were coming along the road, just where we 're sitting now, and they were passing that bit of a rock there—sure, you can see it for yourself—she calls out to them from inside the coffin: "Mind the corner," says she.'

That story seemed to call for something stronger than a sample of the stream that crossed the road, so I opened a bottle and we sat down again.

I asked if the bailiffs gave much trouble in those parts, seeing that they were so low in the social scale of hell.

'Not now,' he said. 'But 'twas different in the old times. Ah, man, they 'd see you starve in those days. Sure, there couldn't help but be bad feeling when the food would be at your door and the children crying for it. I 'll tell you a story now and maybe you wouldn't believe it, but if you was to go up that bhoreen that you see there to the north you 'd find the place where he lived. Spillane was his name, the man I 'm telling you about, though you wouldn't see much but a few stones of the house now, for it 's all tumbled down and the most of it is taken for walls. Spillane was his name, as I told you, and he was a great poacher. He 'd be out every night of the week, and every day of the week, and the bailiffs would be daft mad to catch him. But he was as fast on his feet as he was fast in his head, and they never caught him or got near him. And he had a black setter bitch, and when he went out after the grouse he 'd tie a bit of a white towel around her belly and maybe another bit round her neck, and from a distance, d'ye see, you'd think it was a black-and-white dog that he had.

'Well, one day one of the bailiffs—a Scotch fellow he was, they always had Scotch on the big estates—came up with him on a narrow ledge of rock overight a cliff and they had a fight and the bailiff was thrown and, begod, he rolled over the edge and was killed. So after a while the constabulary came along, and they arrested Spillane and they arrested the setter, and they took the two of them away to jail and they were brought up for trial in Tralee, the two of them together. But the police were in a great fix because no one had seen a black setter on the hills that day when the fight happened. 'Twas only a black-and-white dog they'd seen. So the jury disagreed. Well, then, after a while they were brought up for trial in Limerick, and the jury disagreed again. And then after a long while they were brought up again in Dublin, and didn't the jury disagree again. So, after three trials, Spillane was free, and so was the setter. But in all the long while they'd been in jail the setter was crossed by another. He belonged to one of the jailers—a fine pedigree dog he was—so by the time Spillane stepped out of the train 'twasn't one dog that was following him but twelve, for she'd had a litter of eleven. And wasn't every single one of them black all but a one, and that black and white. He sold every one of the black ones for three pounds each, for they were great stock, don't you see, and he made thirty pounds on the lot. But the black-and-white one he kept. "No man will ever take her from me," he said.'

CHAPTER FIFTEEN

SOON AFTER DAWN next morning I continued on my way into the valley and up the winding road over the Tim Healy Pass to the southern shore of the Kenmare River, as terrifying and splendid a corkscrew drive as the journey from La Guaira to Caracas in Venezuela. In both one looks up from below and wonders by what disruption of the laws of physics one will ever reach the upper rung of that tortuous ladder cut in the mountainside. But there is little similarity between the two landscapes, for the peaks of Venezuela are clean chiselled from the heavens and the red soil of their slopes is parched under an impenitent sky, while in the Healy Pass range succeeds range of misty hills, lost and found in their enveloping clouds.

Beyond those sterile hills in Venezuela one finds a city sparkling white in a wealth of vivid green. Houses are shaded by tall trees festooned with orchids; oleanders and hibiscus border the roads. On the Kerry side of the Healy Pass there is no city, but there is the same vivid green, the roads are lined with the crimson of fuchsia hedges and the woods sing with the splendour of rhododendrons, while overhead against the light the colours of the copper beeches rise in a crescendo from pale amber to deepest burgundy.

From Kenmare—*Ceann-mara*, the head of the sea—my road took me along the northern shore of the estuary. Gannets soaring high shone silver in the early sunlight; the dark head of a seal appeared and disappeared, close in to the shore.

There seemed more stray animals than usual on the road that morning: cattle and sheep, pigs, donkeys. To me, cows on the road always suggest innocence and thoughtfulness; they make no attempt whatever to get out of your way, being quite content to stand and gaze in contemplation through your windscreen. Sheep, on the other hand, always fearful and ready to panic, must have guilty consciences. Pigs have perfect manners; they know their place on the side of the road, and with a fine natural dignity keep to it. A donkey has too much humility; it stands in the middle of your course until the very last moment, as if waiting to say: 'Why, of course I 'll move.' Ganders are insolent. Hens are crassly stupid. Guinea fowl are just silly.

I reached Miss O'Flaherty's hotel at West Cove, beyond Sneem, in time for breakfast, and then because I 'd made an early start I stayed on for lunch, and then, with the warmth of the afternoon, it seemed a pity not to wait for supper, and after that I remembered that it was still cold in the mornings so I said I 'd sleep indoors, and eventually I stayed for a week.

The country all around that part of the coast is a mass of rocks, boulders, stones, bogs, and heather. Here and there a small holding of a few acres, here and there a cottage with a scrap or two of cultivated soil. Towering above all, mountains rough with the corrugations of time.

'You wouldn't find lovelier country anywhere in the

world, I'm sure,' said Miss O'Flaherty. 'With the hills behind us changing their colours every moment and the sea before us never the same, what more could you want to look at?' I agreed with her. With a deluge of flowers in her garden and wild birds tame about the house, her world seemed 'paradise enow.'

One afternoon, in a small bay not far from the hotel, I found a sand boat with bow ashore, fully loaded, waiting for the tide to refloat her. In the morning on a falling tide she had been run aground, and during the day her crew had filled her with sand. Now the three men were sitting on the grass at the head of the beach. They would be taking the sand to Kilmakilloge, twenty miles up the estuary.

While we were talking one of the three fetched a fiddle from the boat and began to play. Hardly had he sounded his first notes than a girl, about twenty years of age, came bounding over the rocks as if from nowhere.

'Give us *The Blackbird*, Flurry,' she said. 'Go on now, and *The Stack of Barley*. Them's my two favourites.'

Flurry paid no attention to her, continuing with the rather dreary lament he had begun.

She sat down on the grass beside him.

'Ah, go on, Flurry, give us something faster.'

Flurry paid no attention.

'Give us *The Drunken Piper*, Flurry. That's grand and fast,' she said, sitting a little closer.

'Faith then, if it's fast play you want I'll give it to you quick enough,' said Flurry, laying his fiddle on the ground and making to get up.

The girl was on her feet in an instant and away with her around the bay as fast as she could run, dodging and swerving, with Flurry after her. Three times they coursed the sand, he almost within touching distance. Then as they came

near us for the fourth time the girl dropped to the ground and sat panting beside the fiddle. Flurry, standing over her, smiled. Then he too sat down, picked up the fiddle, and gave her the tunes she had asked for.

As he played, a pair of oyster-catchers on a weed-covered rock some fifty yards from the shore were walking round each other with their necks thrust forward and their bills pointed downwards, piping their mating notes. And while this dual courtship proceeded, an ass-cart with a high, red crib was driven on to the sand and into the water axle deep, beside a rowing-boat filled with turf. The donkey who, poor fellow, had been robbed of all desire but for food, stood quietly in the water while its owner transferred the turf from the boat. Then, struggling through the water and the soft sand, it pulled its load up a winding lane and disappeared behind the hill. Half an hour later the incoming tide lifted the sand boat and presently, with her three tanned sails filled by the westerly wind, she was heading up the estuary.

About three miles to the east of Miss O'Flaherty's, among the mountains, stands Staigue Fort, considered by authorities to be one of the most perfect of the ancient forts in Ireland. Though the knoll on which it is built is dwarfed by the surrounding hills, the fort within its fosse and with a stream on either side occupied a strong position. Some thirty yards in diameter, its circular wall is more than thirteen feet thick at the base, tapering to seven feet at its highest point, which is about eighteen feet from the ground. Though individual stones of the wall are not so large as those in the great forts on Aran, the outside face of the building has the same splendid finish, showing no sign of a tool and unimpaired by time. In striking contrast to this outer simplicity the whole inner structure of the wall consists of intersecting flights of steps, ten pairs of them, so constructed that they follow the tapering of the masonry. The defenders would have had easy access to the rampart.

In the mountains behind West Cove in a lonely valley is the cave of St. Crohane. It was one day when the saint was riding through this valley on his white horse that he was attacked by an evil spirit. The frightened horse backed in against the rock and the rock gave way behind it. To this day you can see the shape of the hindquarters of the horse, six feet deep in the rock, and above it on either side the marks of the elbows of the saint as he too pressed backwards into the stone.

There is a well near the saint's birthplace at the foot of the Dunkerron Mountains where many get healed of their sickness, especially those who see 'a small little trout in the water.' There is another well near the grave of the saint at Coad, known as 'the Well of the Cures'—'the water in it would never boil for you'—and there on 30th July people perform rounds and take a sip of the water. After the religious duties of the day, 'the night is a great one altogether for the young people. There 's some do say that the saint must be a great boozer and a great boxer, too, for the lads drink heavy and then settle up all their old differences in the ring.'

One day during my stay at West Cove the weather turned

cold and blustery.   It was little pleasure to be out of doors.
'By the look of you,' said Miss O'Flaherty that evening,
''twould do you good to have a walk.   Slip down and have a
chat with my sister at the Mountain Dew.'

So, ever obedient to a woman's word, I walked the mile
into Castle Cove.   It was a dirty night, but as I went along
I could hear a snipe drumming, high overhead.   At the
best of times it is difficult to place such a bird in its aerial
antics, but with the echo from the nearby hills it was well-
nigh impossible.   'I'll find it coming back,' I thought.
But, coming back, the man I happened to be walking with
insisted that there were several snipe in the air.

'Isn't it natural,' he said, 'for them to be after the same
little bird below in the bog, she with the glint in her eye,
waiting.   The same thing just is happening with the boys
in the village beyond.   'Tis the eye that does it.   Never
mind the legs or the bill.'

Two old men were sitting by the bar on the right of the
shop when I went in; an old woman was sitting on the left
beside the counter, with a basket of groceries on her lap.

'Here's the very man now will tell you the truth,' said
Miss O'Flaherty's sister as I went in.   'Denis Cotter here
was saying there was trees would give you milk and there was
animals that laid eggs, and Jerry was saying it couldn't be.'

'It's true,' I said.   'I've drunk the milk from the coco-nut
tree and I've seen animals that lay eggs—turtles, they call
them.   And there are others that do it too, crocodiles
and snakes.'

Then I told them of the kiwi in New Zealand, a bird without wings or tail and no bigger than a hen that lays an egg
twice the size of a goose's.

'Sure, that would be a miracle,' said the old woman by the
counter.

'Would you believe it, Mary?' asked Miss O'Flaherty.

'Maybe 'tis sometimes easier to believe than to go looking for the evidence,' said Mary.

The door opened and a girl with two men came in.   I was introduced to Miss Main of the hotel at Ballinskelligs.

'That's a place you should visit,' said Miss O'Flaherty.

'You can see every mountain in Kerry from there,' said Denis.

'And could I get to the Skelligs?' I asked.

'You could, to be sure,' said Miss Main.   'I'd fix it for you.'

'Isn't it a pity you're not going earlier in the year,' said Miss O'Flaherty, 'and maybe taking someone with you.'

''Tis too late,' said Denis.   'Shrove is the only time for Skellig.'

When, centuries ago, the Irish Church agreed to conform to the Roman rule for the date of Easter, there were still some monks living in out-of-the-way places who adhered to the old ways, whereby Easter fell from eight to fifteen days later than under the new rule.   What was good enough for St. Patrick, they said, was good enough for them, and what right, said they, had pope or prelate to interfere with the teachings of St. Patrick?   Therefore it happened that on islands like the Skelligs the date of Easter fell later than elsewhere, and those couples on the mainland who by accident or otherwise had been unable to get married before midnight on Shrove Tuesday could still cross over to the island and celebrate their nuptials before the penitential season of Lent. Out of all this there grew the idea that for spinsters and bachelors the last hope was on the Skelligs.   I myself can remember the times when 'Skellig Lists' were printed and published in Cork, giving in doggerel form and often none too politely the names of couples who might thus succeed.

Sometimes probable matches were heralded; more often the fun lay in the incongruity of the pairs mentioned. To-day, except for the lighthouse keepers, there are no human inhabitants on the islands, but the oratories and cells of the monastery, whose history goes back twelve centuries or more, remain in splendid preservation, five hundred feet sheer above the sea. Though the old joke persists and an occasional list is composed, there are no longer any amenities for tardy lovers.

CHAPTER SIXTEEN

A FEW DAYS LATER I reached Ballinskelligs. My sister-in-law, Patience Empson, who was on a short visit to Ireland, had joined me. 'Mind the paint pots,' she said as we drove through the gates of Main's Hotel. 'And the mattresses,' she added as we turned towards the front door.

'Don't be looking at all that,' said Miss Main as she welcomed us. 'It's a good time of year for a clean up.'

Next morning we took a walk along the shore. 'You'll find Paddy Mac below at the pier,' said Miss Main as we set out. 'He says he'll take you to the Skelligs the first fine day.'

'If it's a good day we'll go to-morrow,' said Paddy when we found him. ''Tisn't so easy to land on them Skelligs without you'd have the wind from the south.'

We had met him not at the pier but near the old monastery which stands all too close to the sea on the western shore of Ballinskelligs Bay. Storms batter on the ruined walls and gnaw at the surrounding graveyard. Long bones protrude from the eroded cliff, and on the foreshore the broken craniums of many who once walked those shores are daily ground to smaller pieces.

'There's plenty from here joins the navy,' said Paddy as we watched a fragment of a skull being lifted by the flooding tide.

Over our heads a pair of choughs were wheeling, uttering their querulous cries: 'Chee-ow! Chee-ow!' and the nearer we came to the monastery the more discordant grew their notes. Inside the building, in a recess about ten feet from

the ground, we found their nest, an untidy mass of twigs and roots, lined with fine grasses, threads of frayed rope and sheeps' wool. It held four eggs, cream coloured, blotched and mottled with grey and brown.
Though the chough is now a rare bird in England, thanks to egg collectors, it is still common on the south and west coasts of Ireland. There, about the cliffs, one sees them constantly, in pairs or in flocks, banking and wheeling, all the time clamorous. In Cornwall, where the birds still survive, it is believed that when King Arthur was killed in battle beside the River Camel his spirit  entered a chough, and that when the day appointed shall have come he will resume his human form and recover his kingdom.

> 'And mark yon bird of sable wing,
>   Talons and beak all red with blood,
> The spirit of the long-lost king
>   Passed in that shape from Camlan's flood.'

Many people in Ireland to-day pronounce chough, as in old English, to rhyme with plough, and from its cry this would certainly seem more appropriate than its modern equivalent: 'chuff.'

That evening, when wandering among the clumps of gorse, the clusters of willows, and the pools of kingcups that chequer the rough grazing land behind the shore-line, we wondered about the morrow's weather. So many people had emphasized to us the difficulty of making a landing on the Great Skellig. Paddy Mac had said that he thought the sky looked good, but added: 'You can no more tell the weather

here than the way a bird will fly.' We remembered Patty
Cronin at Gougane and the snail that foretold a successful
day. We wished that he was with us to pronounce another
augury. Then, as we stepped from among some yellow
iris on to the close-cropped grass of a dune, we saw before
us what might be termed a scatteration of snails: golden
shells and silver shells on purple stones, lavender and lemon
and blue on emerald leaves; large shells and small shells,
some veined white on plum colour, some veined crimson
on white. It was difficult to walk without stepping on them.

Next morning, whatever the snails may have portended,
the weather was perfect—a clear sky and a gentle breeze from
the south. We sailed at noon. Seals slid into the water
from the rocks as we passed close to the cliffs; razorbills and
guillemots were everywhere about us, diving and preening and
sitting up in the water to flap their wings. We threw out lines
for pollack and caught three. Then, rounding Bolus Head, we
saw the Skelligs, like two tall sailing ships, ten miles to the west.

The nearer we came to the rocks, the greater the number
of gannets that flew over our heads, some soaring high, others
fishing, dropping like a plummet from a hundred feet or more
above the water. One of them, on the surface in the line of
our approach, was unable to rise until it had disgorged a large
fish. Many of the birds were flying towards the smaller
island with long strands of seaweed trailing far behind them
from their beaks.

'You 'd need armour on you to get ashore there,' said Paddy to Patience when she suggested a landing on the Little Skellig. 'You 'd be destroyed if you put one foot on the place without tin plates about your legs. Them birds have beaks like a harpoon.'

Patience agreed with him on that point. She had visited the gannetry at Cape Kidnappers in New Zealand, and knew what it meant to be attacked by dagger-like beaks. But she was anxious to get ashore and compare the two colonies. She remembered the elaborate greeting ceremony that occurred between each pair when one of them returned from the sea to take its turn on the nest: the stretching up of the heads and the rubbing together of the beaks, the bowing, the mutual preening. Sometimes, without waiting for its partner, a bird on the nest would rise and perform a solo dance, lifting its wings and bowing, dipping its head under a wing repeatedly while all the time squawking loudly. This would be an incentive to the birds on neighbouring nests to do the same. For a while there would be turmoil and then, their emotions subsiding, they would settle down and be quiet again. With birds as with humans, mood is infectious.

Dr. Fraser Darling, after long observations of gulls and other sea birds, has much to say about the psychological effect of communal activity on the individuals of a colony. In his book, *Bird Flocks*, he tells how the behaviour of any one bird may have a stimulating effect on the other birds near by, and how eventually this may lead to a group potency to breed. Where numbers are few and sufficient stimulus is not created, there will be nests but no eggs. May not this have its parallel among primitive people who, lacking other stimuli, find achievement through the ritual dance?

As we circled the island it was all too obvious that, even if we did manage to get on to a ledge of rock, it would be impossible to climb further. ''Tisn't a place you could set a foot unless you were a bird,' said Paddy Mac. From the water-line to the topmost peak, every ledge and shelf, every possible foothold, was crowded with gannets: white streams of them seemed to pour over the crest and flow down the steep sides. Everywhere there was clamour and movement, birds coming and going, posturing, mating, squabbling. We dropped our sail and made our way close in to the tall buttresses of rock. Over our heads was a canopy of soaring birds, sparkling white against the blue of the sky. Through our glasses we could see the young ones feeding, plunging their heads into the parents' mouths to receive the regurgitated food. We could see, too, the returning birds laying their offerings of weed before their mates on the nests. Then would follow the bowing and the posturing and the rubbing together of beaks, and finally the change-over on the nest.

It seems an odd thing that a feature so hard and tough as a gannet's beak should be capable of emotional response, yet Fraser Darling noticed the same capacity in the antlers of a stag which, at one moment utilized as weapons of attack, at the next are sensitive to the most delicate stimuli.

'Billing' is not uncommon in the love-making of birds. Puffins indulge in bouts of it as a prelude to further activity; likewise the razorbill and the black guillemot. Ravens hold each other's beaks in prolonged endearment, and the nebbing of parrakeets is well known. I have seen chaffinches caressing each other thus during the moment of their ecstasy.

It is two miles from Little Skellig to Skellig Michael, the larger of the twin islands and dedicated to the patron saint of high places, like St. Michael's Mount in Cornwall and again in Normandy. When we were beside the smaller island we were conscious only of gannets; as we approached the larger one our interest veered to kittiwakes. Packed on the ledges, tier upon tier, they gave to the rock face the appearance of a Cambodian temple sculptured in low relief.   And here and there among the gulls, whose dove-grey backs were turned towards the sea to ensure cleanliness of the nests, were the darker forms of guillemots and razorbills.   The cup-like nests of the kittiwakes, built of seaweed and thrift, held one or two pale grey eggs blotched with brown; the single egg, bright green or ochreous, of the guillemot rested on bare rock.

It was the calmest day of the year, we were told, so calm that the twelve months' supply of coal had come to the lighthouse keepers from the mainland.   There was no trouble in getting it ashore, neither was there any trouble for us: we just stepped on to the small concrete landing stage.

Two hundred feet above sea level is the lighthouse, guarded by a massive wall.   'You 'd want strong walls in the winter,' said one of the keepers, 'with the spray coming over you like the ocean.'   And three hundred and fifty feet above the lighthouse on a small plateau is the 'monastery.'   It consists of two small oratories and six beehive cells, and there is also the remains of a church of more recent construction.

The oratories and the cells were built without mortar, each layer of stones overlapping the course below it towards the centre so that eventually only a small flat stone was needed to close the hole at the top.   Here in these wind-pierced shelters a community of monks lived their lives of poverty, chastity, and obedience, following the rule of St. Pachome, the founder of monastic life.   He it was who, early in the fourth century, when living as a hermit in a deserted village on the east bank of the Nile, determined that those who came to him for spiritual guidance should dwell as one community and observe the same rule.   Hitherto anchorites had practised poverty and chastity only, now they were called upon to obey.   It was the beginning of monasticism.

K

St. Pachome preached not only abstinence but self-restraint. It is related that when visiting a monastery in the desert and finding little food set upon the table, he rebuked the cook, not because there was insufficient to eat but because, there being no more than sufficient, the brethren lacked opportunity for restraint. 'I truly wish,' he said, 'to have food in abundance cooked daily and set before the brethren, so that in practising abstinence every day, and in restraining themselves from partaking of what hath been given to them, they may make an addition daily to their spiritual excellence.'

On the Skelligs it would have been a very ingenious cook who could have set abundance of food daily before the brethren. How they found a bare sufficiency is hard to imagine. Fish there may have been in plenty, and the eggs of sea birds for a short season in the year, but little else beside brackish water from the two wells. Perhaps a few goats were kept for milk, perhaps a little grain was grown on the fragment of level ground. Perhaps, too, like the people living on the coast at that time, the monks had a dispensation which allowed them to eat the flesh of puffins in Lent and on 'other meagre days,' the argument being that as these birds live exclusively on fish their flesh must be of the same nature as fish. But apart from the exercise of accentuated restraint those in the monastery, hearing no sound from the outer world but 'the chant of the waves on their eternal course,' would have had ample opportunity to practise the austerities, the discipline, and the self-abnegation of the Pachomian rule.

In spite of the severity of their lives, many of the early Desert Fathers lived to extreme old age. There are records that some were still vigorous at eighty, eighty-five, and ninety years of age. A few lived to be over a hundred, among them St. Anthony, 'held in abundant esteem by St. Pachome and reciprocating those feelings,' who died at the age of one hundred and five, 'healthy to the last, not a tooth dropped.'

To reach the Skellig monastery from the lighthouse there are six hundred steps zigzagging perilously up the cliff, and if one would visit the last 'station' there is yet another climb. This time it is along the narrow crest of a spur whose sides slope almost vertically to the sea. At the extremity of that ridge, a stone with a cross incised upon it projects twelve feet into space. There, poised seven hundred feet above the sea, the devout pilgrim kneels and prays.

I did not attempt to scale those heights. Instead, I was content at lower levels to watch the puffins rocketing to and from their nesting holes among the tussocks of pink thrift. From the sanctuary of rabbit burrows and from under slabs of rock they shot into the air like small torpedoes. When I looked into a burrow, there would be no sign of the bird's body, only two large white disks from which a pair of small eyes gazed, unblinking.

In contrast to the dignified and purposeful flight of a gannet, every movement and gesture of a puffin seems intended as a joke. Their expression is at all times quizzical, reminiscent of clowns who after performing some strange antic look at you with pained surprise that you should show any sign of wonder. The stance of these birds, their walk, their run, even their flight when landing or taking off with scarlet feet spread wide, is pantomimic; and yet as Richard Perry, an acute observer, has written of them: 'One cannot imagine a structural body more perfectly evolved and adapted to its several environments in its five dimensions under and on the sea, under and on the ground, and in the air.'

There have been many strange beliefs connected with these islands. A history of Kerry, published in 1756, says of Skellig Michael that 'no bird hath the power to fly over that part of it where the chapels and walls stand, without first alighting on the ground, which they walk gently over, and then take wing.' It is told that fishermen of an evening have seen the souls of the dead hovering over the islands when on their way to Tir na n-Og, the Land of Perpetual Youth. I had found similar traditions in the Pacific islands. In Samoa, Pulotu, the Land of the Departed, lies to the west, and early voyagers in canoes far out at sea have met with the souls of those who had already died: 'some were weeping, some were laughing, others were singing or playing on instruments'; in Pulotu they would find the lake whose water confers immortality. At Rarotonga in the Cook Islands I was shown on the western shore the stone whence the spirits of the dead set out for Pulotu, and a priest-doctor there told me that if one had sufficient *mana* it was possible to catch these souls and restore them to their human bodies. Of Spirits Bay, which faces to the west from the most northerly point of New Zealand, there are similar tales, and again at the Baie des Trépassés in the west of Brittany. Perhaps it was some similar prompting that led those early monks westward to what was then 'the furthest outpost of the known world.'

CHAPTER SEVENTEEN

IT WAS ELEVEN O'CLOCK in the morning at Gougane, and Shaun the Post had just arrived. He had put his bicycle against the wall beside the green post-box, and was saying a word to Denny when I came along.

'You 'll be putting a pain in my back with the letters I 'm carrying for you,' he said, turning to me. 'Three and four a day you be getting, and sending out maybe as many. What in the name of God do you be writing about? Aren't you worn out with it all?'

'He 's not losing flesh on it, anyway,' said Denny, prodding my waist line.

'He makes great use of his food,' said Shaun.

137

'You 're no one to talk,' I said to Denny. 'Look at your top button.'

'Sure, you could calve me,' said Denny.

'He could,' said Shaun, 'and chew the cud after.'

'I 'm away off to take exercise,' I said, and with that I left them and walked westwards into the valley.

Beside the roadway foxgloves sprang from every cranny among the rocks, and London pride and pennywort competed for supremacy among the smaller stones. Beyond the dark marshy land speckled with the gentian blue of milkwort and the silver of cotton grass, clusters of royal fern were still unfurling, and beyond the ferns the calm lake among the rugged mountains 'lay like a woman in a warrior's arms.' Crowning her head were white water-lilies, 'the sinless, scentless flowers which blossom at the gates of Paradise.' In Rumania it is believed that all flowers have souls and that the water-lily, because of its purity, will be the ultimate judge of all the others, inquiring of them how when on earth they had used their fragrance.

I left the path and followed a sheep track up the hill-side. Everywhere among the stones and heather and patches of sphagnum moss were the pale green rosettes of butterwort. Apart from London pride—whose name is derived, not from the city of London, but from a Mr. London, who found fame as a gardener in the eighteenth century—these clusters of leaves with their violet-like blossoms are among the most conspicuous flowers of the hill-side. The leaves lie close to the damp soil. The roots are shallow: they do not need to be otherwise, for the plant is carnivorous. Each spoon-shaped leaf has its upper surface covered with thousands of minute glands capable of secreting a sticky fluid. Though not affected by rain or by specks of grit that may drop on them, those glands react immediately to the touch of an insect.

Not only do they then secrete the mucilage, but they pour forth an acid, and at the same time the edges of the leaf curl inwards. The insect, held as on a fly-paper, is soon entombed, and when a few hours later the leaf unfolds, there is little of it to be seen save perhaps the wings and a few remnants of the skeleton. There are few full-grown leaves that do not show such relics.

Instead of mountaineering, as I had intended, I sat on a stone and made a drawing of one of these flowers, and when that was completed I rotated on my pedestal and made another. It was only when I was adding the last touches that I realized the stone on which I had been sitting covered an ants' nest.

Later that day, being restless, I dropped into the house next door. Denny was away in Bantry, Norah was in charge of the bar. Batty Kit was there and Patty Cronin, and Teigue the Pass from Keimaneigh. He didn't often come into the bar—he was not very strong in the purse.

'Wouldn't you sit down,' said Patty to me as I stood by the counter.

'I'd rather stand,' I said. 'I sat on an ants' nest this morning and I'm still burning.'

'Black ants?' asked Patty.

'Black enough,' I said.

'They'll always sting a Protestant,' said Patty. 'They'd never touch a Catholic. 'Tis only the red ones will sting a Catholic, and they'd never harm a Protestant.'

'You should carry a bit of rib-leaf (plantain) in your shoe,' said Teigue, 'and then neither of them will sting you, whatever your persuasion.'

Norah inquired about my visit to the Skelligs. 'We had a fine girl in here last week would have suited you,' she said.

'Who was that?' I asked.

'Bessie the Bull,' she said.

'Sure, there isn't a bed in Ireland would hold the two of them,' said Patty.

'How did she get the name?' I asked.

'Bessie's father was a powerful man,' said Teigue, 'powerful beyond all talking. His bull turned on him one day in the yard and was like to have killed him. Didn't the old man take the beast by the two horns and throw it over his shoulder. It fell on the tip of its nose—you could hear the copper ring strike the stone—and the weight of its quarters broke its neck. 'Tis "Paddy the Bull" he is ever since, and his daughter Bessie after him.'

'And did you travel it all in your van?' Patty asked me.

'All the way to Ballinskelligs, and then by boat,' I said.

'Sure, the world is no more to him than a haggard,' said Batty Kit.

'I never knew Skelligs was a place,' said Teigue. 'I thought 'twas only talk.'

'Were you ever on a ship, Batt?' asked Norah.

'I was,' said Batty. 'I was, faith. 'Twas when I saw off me two sons to America, east beyond at Queenstown—Cove they call it now. 'Tis twenty years since, and there's never been a Christmas without a token from them.'

'Was it a big ship?' asked Norah.

'God Almighty! I was never in such a place in me life, before or since. We went down the stairs and down the stairs until we got lost away below. Where did we finish up but in the kitchen, and would you believe it, there wasn't a woman in the place. 'Twas all men was there, and they with tall white hats on their heads. Basting ducks they were, and on my oath if there was one bird in the oven there was two hundred.'

'You wouldn't get that number in one oven?' said Teigue.

'Begor, you would,' said Batty. 'Wasn't the oven as big as this room, and hadn't it doors on every side of it. The cooks would be walking round and round, kicking the doors open with the toe of their boot and basting the birds with a spoon had an arm on it as long as a shovel.'

'Did they give you a bite to eat?' asked Teigue.

'Begor, they didn't at all,' said Batt.

'Weren't they mean, all the same,' said Patty.

''Twas the way I was frightened the ship would sail off and carry me with her,' said Batt. '"Come on away up out of this," I said to the boys. Begod, we travelled every townland in the ship before we got back to the roof, and when we came out in the wind wasn't there a lake there before us, the same as you 'd see above on Myloch, and the boys and the girls lepping in and diving out.'

A car pulled up outside the open door as we were talking, and from it emerged a big stout man. He came into the bar, looking around him with a serious expression on his face.

'Where 's Denny?' he asked.

'He 's out,' said Norah.

'Is he fishing?'

'He 's shopping.'

'What time will he be back?'

'About eight o'clock.'

'Are you sure?'

'I am.'

The visitor seemed distressed.

'Is it nothing I can do for you?' asked Norah.

The big man leaned close over to her, across the counter. 'Whisper,' said he, 'where would I get a bottle of maggots?'

'I 'll find out for you,' she said. She left the bar and went

through to the back kitchen to inquire.   The big man paced
up and down anxiously.   No, he wouldn't have a drink.

Norah came back.   'Come here,' she said.   'Go inside
in the hall and look under the sofa and you 'll see a canister is
full of them.'

The big man did as he was told.   A few minutes later he
came back beaming.   In his hand was a small flat tin filled
with wriggling maggots.   You 'd think it was snuff the
tender way he handled them.

'I 'll bring you some trout in the morning,' he said to
Norah as he went out of the door.

I left soon afterwards myself.   I was still worried by the
sectarianism of ants.

CHAPTER EIGHTEEN

EARLY IN JUNE my boat, the *Willow*, in which I had lived while writing *Sweet Thames Run Softly*, arrived from England. Now I was free to while away the daylight hours and, as the nights grew warmer, to sleep afloat. 'Isn't she the darling?' they said as we launched her on Gougane lake.

My favourite place on the lake during the day was at its far western end, where behind a screen of rushes I could float unobserved, writing or drawing. There the water was shallow, and looking into it I could see below me the matted leaves of water lobelia. They were already sending up flower stems, and soon their pale lilac blossoms would be as a mist over wide stretches of the lake. Horsetails were there too like hosts of miniature spear-heads springing from the water. With the naked eye it is not easy to realize the delicate moulding of those stalks, but when seen under high magnification they have the grace and symmetry of minarets whose fluted sides, tier upon tier, lead the eye upwards to their summits. Many species of this plant prefer drier habitats but all of them have the power of secreting minute crystals of silica in the cuticle of their stems. One variety at least is so rough that it was at one time known as pewter-wort and was in common use for polishing metal. Within living memory, dairymaids in Yorkshire used the corn horsetail for scouring their milk pails.

At night I would drop anchor in deeper water under shelter of the hill and there, played on by light airs, the *Willow* would swing gently, while the rushes arching overhead wove intricate patterns of intersecting lines, dark against the skies of dusk and dawn. Time and again I would be reminded by

those traceries of how, when floating on the waterways of
Venice, I saw, as grilles, lunettes and railings, scrolls of

metal that were rhythmic as bending reeds.   At one moment I was looking at the iron, at the next, the space that it enclosed.   And when the sun was low and shadows cast by the railings repeated those devices, another motif would be added to the themes of thought.

My most vivid memory of Venice is not of the canals and the gondolas, nor of the Doge's Palace, nor the great square where one in the semblance of Donatello's St. Mark mistook me for St. John; nor of the ornate façade of the great cathedral, but, rather, of the *pavimento* within.   In that mosaic was an infinity of creative delight, expressed in the simplest terms—the basis perhaps of all art.   At one moment the emphasis of the darker stones dominated that of the lighter ones, at the next the dark ones became the background.   Then the pattern made by the two together would hold the attention until it, in its turn, dissolved and a new rhythm caught the eye.

Repetition is one of the cardinal principles of emphasis in art, whether it occurs in the refrain of poetry, in a *corps de ballet*, or in the great Italian altar-pieces where again and again heads and haloes of the saints and the many wings of the angels all compel the eye towards the central figure.   In more recent painting its value is seen in the repeated curves of umbrellas in Renoir's *Les Parapluies*, in the dancers of Seurat's *Chahut*, and in many compositions by Stanley Spencer.

Another kind of repetition occurs in the fifteenth-century engraving, *The Battle of the Gladiators*, by Pollaioulo.   In this the two central figures have an almost identical silhouette, but in one it is the front view of the figure which is contained within the outline while in the other it is the back.   By this form of counterchange the artist has imparted to his design a rhythm not at first detected by the beholder.

Sometimes in my boat I would be reminded of the patterns of reeds carved in low relief on slabs of stone which once adorned the walls of Sennacherib's palace at Nineveh. To-day they embellish the Assyrian Gallery of the British Museum. On these sculptured panels reeds occur again and again in labyrinths of stems and leaves, calm and static foils to the vigours of battle or the chase. In representational art there can be few if any more splendid examples of the value of repetition: palm-trees and vines exquisitely formalized; chariots with their wheels simplified to the cross within a circle, as on many of the gold disks of Ireland already discussed; horses in arrested movement; armies of men suggested by a mere dozen figures.

There was an evening, too, when with the water all around me, a raven croaking on the hill-side and a ring-dove passing overhead, I thought of the clay tablet, found in the ruins of one of those palaces, which tells the Babylonian story of the Flood. It was one of many thousand tablets in the library of Assurbanipal, a man of learning and a patron of literature, a grandson of Sennacherib who built the palace. Its story is a close parallel to the Hebrew version of the Deluge found in the Old Testament, variations between the two arising from the fact that even at that time the legend was an old one in Mesopotamia and scribes allowed their *styli* to accord with local taste or prejudice.

Scientific proof of the Flood was found in 1929 when Sir Leonard Woolley, excavating on the site of Ur of the Chaldees, found at a depth of some sixty feet a stratum of 'clean clay, uniform throughout, the texture of which showed that it had been laid there by water.' In the soil above the clay were pottery, ashes from fires, and other household rubbish; in the soil below these were likewise pots and domestic refuse. But the pots in the lower layer, such as the one I have engraved, were not of the same period as those found above; they belonged to an earlier civilization. The bed of clay represented a break in the continuity of local culture: eight feet in thickness, it implied a prolonged inundation unparalleled in local history.

CHAPTER NINETEEN

'WOULDN'T YOU BE frightened?' asked Mickey Tobin when, during the evening of 23rd June, I mentioned to him that I was going to sleep on the lake that night. 'I wouldn't do it for a thousand pounds,' he said.

'Why not?' I asked.

'It 's Midsummer Night,' he said.

'I have the hazel stick you gave me,' I told him.

'I 'd be frightened all the same,' he said.

The easterly wind had faded when I reached the head of the lake. Momentarily a light breeze ruffled the surface of the water; then it too died away and again there was calm and peace.

There was no darkness that night, just a twilight as the sun took its course to the north, a twilight pierced by the light of fires that blazed on successive hills. From where I lay in my boat I could see on a knoll behind the island figures dancing round a bonfire, and I could hear the music of the fiddles that accompanied them. Then, as the blaze subsided, I saw men, women, and children leaping through the flames, and trails of sparks like comets, as live brands were plucked from the fire and thrown into the air. I remembered how, many years ago, when the people of Knockainy neglected to light the usual Midsummer fires on the Hill of Aine, a fairy princess, they were surprised and alarmed to see the hill ablaze with fires throughout the night.

And while I watched these people celebrating, unconsciously, a pagan rite, I knew that other celebrants were moving on the dark island, this time worshipping in the Christian faith—pilgrims to the shrine of St. Finnbarr, to the

148

cells where he and his monks prayed and fasted twelve centuries ago. Each pilgrim makes a round of the 'stations' before midnight; five prayers at the first cell, ten at the second, fifteen at the third, until at the ninth and last they say forty-five. Further prayers are said at the holy well. Two hours it takes them, and the series must be completed before midnight. Some of the worshippers stay on to do another round after midnight, others keep vigil till the dawn.

I didn't sleep much that night, listening to sounds unknown by day, listening to familiar birds calling with unfamiliar notes, listening to whispers of rustling reeds.

My mind, too, was full of memories of part-forgotten reading; of the bonfires lit in the west of England to bless the orchards, the cartwheels that in Wales and other parts of Europe were bound in straw and sent blazing down hills for divination of the harvest, of cattle being driven between fires in parts of Ireland to ward off disease in the coming year, of bonfires on the hills of Sweden and Russia where, at the Midsummer festival, young folks danced around the fires and leapt through the flames in couples. Even in Peru, at one time, the crests of the Andes would be ablaze with bonfires lit by the Indians in honour of St. John, a custom brought to them no doubt by the Spaniards. Then, as my thoughts came back to personal experience, I remembered a particular festival in which as a boy, at Carrigrohane, I took part. My father had contributed a couple of tar barrels, and all the children of the neighbourhood had spent the afternoon gathering sticks. Many an old gate-post and door found a speedy end in that pile of brushwood. The fire was built at the cross-roads, just outside the 'little gate' of the rectory—the little gate that opened from a footpath bordered on one side by a beech hedge. Boss Payne, our gardener, never tired of trimming that hedge, and my father never tired of admiring it. When the young green was on it in spring, he would take every visitor to see it. It didn't matter that there were flowers galore in the garden—it was the flawless green that appealed to him. 'Oh, man alive, 'tis like velvet,' he would say.

Another feature of the rectory landscape that gave him almost equal pleasure was a bush of berberis that grew on the far side of the gravel sweep in front of the house. It stood about ten feet high and was trimmed each year to a perfect dome. In the spring its vesture of golden blossom gave it an oriental splendour. Nobody on foot or bicycle, in pony trap or motor car, ever came to the hall door without being taken across the gravel to admire it at close quarters.

As I write, a curious incident connected with my father and that gravel occurs to me. It was the night after his death, and I had just arrived from England. The coffin was in the drawing-room at the back of the house, and my two sisters and I were sitting over the fire in the dining-room which overlooked the drive. It was about nine o'clock and dark

when all three of us heard a horse and trap come up the avenue, pass over the loose gravel, and turn into the stable yard. 'It's George Logan,' said my sister Aimée. 'He has been visiting father regularly, and now he's come to see you. He's gone into the yard,' she added. 'When he has put up the horse he'll come in at the back door.'

'I'll go and meet him,' I said, and so saying I went to the back door. But when I opened the door there was no sign of George, horse, or trap, neither was there when I crossed the yard and went into the stable.

On that particular St. John's Eve of which I was telling we had a grand fire. It was so splendid that no horse would pass the cross-roads. Well, what matter? 'Twas only a few miles extra to go round the other way. There was a crowd of people of all ages, and while some of them attended to the fire, throwing on extra fuel, others danced to an accordion. It was great fun to throw a lighted brand high into the air and

watch the sparks that marked its flight.   If it fell in a field
it could only do good.   In many parts of Ireland at that time
it was the custom deliberately to throw the brands into the
fields, believing as in ancient times that it would increase the
crops, though not realizing that it was indeed an offering to
the fire god.

And in the middle of it all, when the higher flames had
subsided and we were jumping through the fire, a solemn,
miserable-looking man came up to my father. 'Have you
forgotten Ezekiel and Jeremiah?' he asked. 'Aren't you
ashamed to be putting your children through the fire to
Moloch?'

'Ah, for goodness' sake, let the innocent children enjoy
themselves,' said my father.

When I awoke in the boat before dawn, the crescent moon
was tipping the low hill to the east.   Soon it was lost in the
glory of the rising sun.   The morning was warm so I slipped
into the lake; then for a while I rejoiced in the cool sunshine.

It was still early when I tied up my boat by the hotel.
Mick Tobin was waiting for me.

'Are you all right?' he asked.

'I'm grand,' I said.

'I've a drop for you here,' he said, handing me a glass of
whiskey. 'I thought you might be wanting something.   Do
you know,' he added, 'Teigue the Pass was for taking his
fiddle along the mountains last night and playing to you from
above.   He said you'd be thinking 'twas fairy music.   But
the boys wouldn't let him.   They said you might do something desperate with the fright that would be on you.'

CHAPTER TWENTY

FUCHSIA HEDGES ARE among the most distinctive features of the countryside in the south and west of Ireland. Mile after mile of roads is lined with their profusion of blossom: crimson, scarlet, or purple, according to the light. And even the verges of the roads and lanes have their lustre of the same colour, for, as with roses, after pollination the petals of the fuchsia fall before they wither.

Like the magnolia, called after Pierre Magnol the botanist, and the dahlia whose name honours the Swedish scientist, Andrew Dahl, so the fuchsia was named after Leonard Fuchs, one of the sixteenth-century fathers of botany in Germany. It was not he, however, who introduced the plant to Europe, but one Captain Firth who brought it to England from South America in 1788.

Ireland should be grateful to Chile for this embellishment of her roads, though Chile would probably look upon the gift as but a small return for Ireland's benefaction to her. It was none other than an O'Higgins who, for his services to Chile in their War of Independence against Spain, was elected first president of the new republic in 1818. That first president, Don Bernardo O'Higgins, was the son of Don Ambrosio, viceroy of Peru. Don Ambrosio was born in County Sligo, and as Ambrose O'Higgins, a barefoot boy, he was glad to earn an odd copper when and how he could. Like many another lad at that time, he contrived to leave Ireland and reach Cadiz, there to join the Spanish Army. Later he went to Lima in Peru where, after keeping a small shop for a while, he took to engineering and eventually prospered in Santiago. At the time of his death he was not only viceroy of Peru but a marquis in the Spanish peerage. It was his son Bernard who is regarded in Chile as one of the country's greatest heroes. His name is written large as that of a province on the map; there is a statue of him in Valparaiso and another in Santiago. Even luxury hotels have been called after him.

Fuchsias came from the lower slopes of the Andes to enrich the flora of Europe, and from a small island a few hundred miles west of those slopes came Robinson Crusoe to enrich English literature. There is no need to repeat the story of how, on 2nd February 1709, a boat which was sent ashore at Mas-a-tierra in the Juan Fernandez Islands by Captain Woodes Rogers, commanding the frigate *Duke*, 320 tons, returned not only with abundance of crawfish but 'with a Man cloth'd in Goat-skins, who look'd wilder than the first Owners of them'—Alexander Selkirk, born in the county of Fife in Scotland, and 'bred a Sailor from his Youth.'

Captain Joshua Slocum, the first man to sail round the world alone and who must surely have known the fears of solitude, having called at Mas-a-tierra in 1896, wondered why Selkirk ever wished to leave the island with its fertile valleys, well-wooded hills, and streams of pure water; no serpents and no wild beasts other than pigs and goats. But then Mas-a-tierra was not uninhabited when Slocum called there, and he was free to leave it when he chose, weather permitting. Unlike Selkirk, it was at sea that *he* experienced solitude.

Selkirk's life afloat during the four months immediately after his rescue must have seemed to him a strange contrast to his four years' loneliness ashore, for not only was he concerned directly or indirectly with the capture of nine ships as 'prizes,' but he also took a leading part in the capture of

Guayaquil. From the day when he was taken on board the *Duke*, though at that time 'he had so much forgot his Language for want of Use, that . . . he seem'd to speak his words by halves,' he held none but positions of rank, either as mate of one of the ships of the ever-increasing fleet or as commander of one of the smaller prizes. At the assault on Guayaquil, he and another man named Connely, presumably from Ireland, were so civil to 'above a Dozen handsom genteel young Women well dress'd' whose jewels they were plundering, that 'the Ladies offer'd to dress 'em Victuals, and brought 'em a Cask of good Liquor.' In an attempt to save their jewels the ladies had concealed them under their clothes, 'but the Gentlewomen in these hot Countries being very thin clad with Silk and fine Linnen,' the despoilers had only to press with their hands on the outside of the ladies' apparel and then through their interpreter modestly request that the jewels be taken off and surrendered. Captain Woodes Rogers, having emphasized in his diary the gallantry of this behaviour, adds: 'Being young Men, I was willing to do 'em this Justice, hoping the Fair Sex will make 'em a grateful Return when we arrive in *Great Britain*, on account of their civil behaviour to these charming Prisoners.'

It would seem that Selkirk at any rate was, to some extent, repaid, for soon after his return to Scotland, when wandering on the hills, lonesome for his island, he met a girl who, if not lonesome, was at any rate alone. He persuaded her to elope with him and he made a will in her favour. Sad to relate, a few years later he forgot both her and the will and left the little he had to another woman, a widow, who in the meantime he had married. I suppose four and a half years' solitude is bound to affect a man's memory.

It is well known that in writing *The Life and Strange Adventures of Robinson Crusoe* Defoe did not adhere strictly to the facts related by Alexander Selkirk. Nobody minds that. In fact, we are indebted to him, for, as Henry James might have said, by altering facts he created truth. But it is not so well known that, almost in those same waters, an event occurred rather more than a century later which became the central theme of another masterpiece, Melville's *Moby Dick*. It was on 20th November 1820 that the whale ship *Essex*, after visiting Juan Fernandez and while cruising to the west of the Galapagos, was attacked by a sperm-whale and sunk. As a result the crew, in three open boats, set out to reach the coast of South America. One of the boats disappeared and was never heard of again; a second was picked up off the coast of Chile with but two men alive. The crew of the third, after ninety-three days at sea, was rescued almost within sight of Crusoe's island. That particular boat was commanded by Owen Chase, first mate of the *Essex*, and among the oddments that he had managed to save from the wreck were 'some eight or ten sheets of writing paper and a lead pencil.' With these he 'commenced to keep a sort of journal,' and from these eight or ten sheets of spray-splashed paper sprang the six hundred odd pages of Melville's *Moby Dick*.

Woodes Rogers's last port of call before his great adventuring was Cork, whence he sailed on 1st September 1708. While in the harbour he recruited a number of men as additions to his crew with whom, he tells us, he was well pleased. If he says nothing of the amenities of that 'very safe anchorage for ships' (is not 'Statio Bene Fida Carinis' the motto of the city?) it can only be because his mind was preoccupied. He tells us: 'Our Crew were continually marrying whilst we staid at Cork, tho they expected to sail immediately.'

We are, however, not short of other distinguished testimony to the great roadstead. In *The Travels of Mirza Abu*

Taleb Khan, during the years 1799–1803, written by himself in the Persian language and translated in 1810 by Professor Stewart, we find: 'The bay resembles a round basin, sixteen miles in circumference. On its shore is situated the town, which is built in the form of a crescent, and defended at each end by small forts. On one side of the bay a large river, resembling the Ganges, disembogues itself; this river extends a great way inland, and passes by the city of Cork. The circular form of this extensive sheet of water, the verdure of the hills, the comfortable appearance of the town on one side, and the formidable aspect of the forts, and so many large ships lying securely in the harbour, conveyed to my mind such sensations as I had never before experienced; and although in the course of my travels I had an opportunity of seeing the Bay of Genoa and the Straits of Constantinople, I do not think either of them is to be compared to this.' Then he tells how in the afternoon they landed in the town and went to the post office to dispatch letters. 'The mistress of the house, being of a hospitable disposition, insisted upon our staying to dinner, and, assisted by her sons and daughters, waited upon us at table. . . . When we were about to return to our ship we wished to pay for our dinner, as is the custom in Europe, but our hostess would not accept a farthing.' He remarks that 'the conduct and appearance of this amiable woman astounded me; she had been the mother of twenty-three children, eighteen of whom were living . . . notwithstanding which she had not the appearance of old age, and I should not have supposed her more than thirty.'

Less than fifty years after His Highness visited Cork, Her Majesty Queen Victoria wrote in her diary: 'On board the *Victoria and Albert*, in the Cove of Cork. The harbour is immense though the land is not very high, and entering by twilight it had a very fine effect.' Whereas the river reminded the Persian prince of the Ganges, to Her Majesty it recalled the Tamar.

It was on the occasion of this royal visit to Cork that, among the many triumphal arches and decorations erected in the queen's honour of which she wrote, 'Nothing could be more gratifying or agreeable,' the *pièce de resistance* was a harp studded with new potatoes. It is said the queen stood up in her carriage to see it more clearly.

CHAPTER TWENTY-ONE

I T IS A LITTLE surprising when travelling through the
Dingle Peninsula, where prehistoric forts and early Christian
monuments confront one at almost every bend of the road,
and where in many districts it is difficult to find an inhabitant
who speaks English, to see in large letters over the door of a
public-house, THE SOUTH POLE—TOM CREAN.

'Faith, then, Tom wrote his own epitaph,' said a native of
the village. 'Wasn't he on three voyages to the Pole?
Wasn't it him was one of the last three saw Captain Scott
alive—himself and a fellow called Lashley, another petty
officer, and Evans a lieutenant—he's some sort of an
admiral now.'

When Crean returned to his native village after long service in the British Navy, which included three expeditions to
the Antarctic, he built himself this pub in the village of
Anascaul and there he lived until his death in 1938. With
his wife, 'Nell the Pole,' he did a thriving business. 'She
was a grand woman behind the bar,' I was told. When,
after hours, they'd be calling for pints, 'two pints here, and
two pints there,' and she'd become moidered with the
calling, she'd say to her daughter: 'For the love of God,
Nelly, shut the door and open the window and let the noise

go down the river.'   Not that the guards were unreasonable, but what else could they do sometimes, 'with the black cloud of discipline hanging over them.'

Tom Crean had been in the Antarctic with Scott in the *Discovery*, 1901–4.   He was with him again in the *Terra Nova* in 1910, and was one of the last supporting party on that tragic expedition.   He was among the few who, eight months later, found Scott with Wilson and Bowers dead in their tent, some seven hundred and fifty miles on their homeward journey from the Pole, with only another eleven miles between them and the next depot.

He sailed again with Shackleton in 1914, and, marooned on an ice-floe, saw the *Endurance* rear up her stern before 'the ice closed over her for ever.'

It was of this man that Scott wrote in his journal: 'Crean is perfectly happy, ready to do anything and go anywhere, the harder the work, the better.'   An earlier entry records: 'An event of Christmas was the production of a family by Crean's rabbit.   She gave birth to seventeen, it is said, and Crean has given away twenty-two!'   It was Crean who, having pulled Lashley out of a crevasse into which he had fallen on his birthday, wished him 'many happy returns.'

Some twenty miles west of the South Pole one reaches the end of the Dingle Peninsula, where within a few miles of the mainland can be seen 'the Blaskets.'   It was from these small and isolated islands, the largest not more than three miles in length and with a total population at that time of a couple of hundred souls, that there came two of the loveliest books ever written about Ireland.   Both were originally in Irish, and both are straightforward narratives of the daily lives of their authors.   Let me quote a few passages from *The Islandman*, by Tomas O'Crohan, translated by Robin Flower.

The old man's aim in writing his story was 'to set down the character of the people about me so that some record of us might live after us, for the like of us will never be again.' He knew that with more and more young people leaving the islands for the mainland the old way of life was sinking into the sea. In 1950, scarce twenty-five years since he wrote his book, the population has dwindled to less than thirty and only one of the islands is inhabited. His book has a background of terrific reality. Not one word in it is said for effect; not one word is needed to heighten the effect.

Speaking of himself as a child, the last of a family of six, he tells us: 'They were all grown up when I was a baby. Nobody expected me at all when I came their way. I am the scrapings of the pot, the last of the litter. When I was at the breast there was little strength in her milk, and beside that I was "an old cow's calf," not easy to rear.'

Telling of his school days and early manhood, he says: 'A potful of boiled potatoes, fish and milk with them, we gobbled down our bellyful of them, young and old. As for tea, nobody in the island in those days had ever seen a kettle, or for long after . . . I lived for a long time from my young days on two meals a day. I 'd have a lot of work done on strand or hill or in the field, and the cows would be coming to milking when I 'd be thinking about taking my morning meal. The sun would be far down in the west when I had the evening meal.' His main occupation at that time was fishing, with intervals ashore for saving turf and work in the fields. There would be an occasional expedition in search of seals, whose flesh was as highly esteemed as pork. Seal oil was employed for light, but 'they didn't put much of that in the cressets, for they used to gulp it down themselves, dipping their bread of Indian meal in it, and they needed it badly enough. I was well in the teens, I think, while this

kind of light was still in use.   The cresset was a little vessel, shaped like a boat or canoe, with one or two pointed ends, three or four feet to it, and a little handle to grip sticking out of its side—the whole thing about eight or ten inches long. The fish or seal oil was put into it, the reed or wick was dipped in the oil and passed over the pointed end of the cresset, and as it burnt away, it was pushed out.   The pith of the rush formed the wick, and often they used a soft twine of cotton or linen for it.   They would often use a large shell instead of a cresset for a light.'

He finishes his book with these words: 'Since the first fire was kindled in this island none has written of his life and his world.   I am proud to set down my story and of the story of my neighbours.   This writing will tell how the Islanders lived in the old days.   My mother used to go carrying turf when I was eighteen years of age.   She did it that I might go to school, for rarely did we get a chance of schooling.   I hope in God that she and my father will inherit the Blessed Kingdom; and that I and every reader of this book after me will meet them in the Island of Paradise.'

The Islandman was written by an old man looking back: Maurice O'Sullivan wrote *Twenty Years a-Growing* with, as it seemed, the greater part of his life before him.   It is sad to think that in the year in which I write the sea has claimed him.   He wrote his book solely for the entertainment of his friends and with no thought that it would reach a wider public.

While still a child Maurice made his first crossing between the mainland and the island. Was there ever a better description of seasickness than this? 'The curragh was mounting the waves, then down again on the other side, sending bright jets of foam into the air every time she struck the water. I liked it well until we were in Mid Bay. Then I began to feel my guts going in and out of each other, and as the curragh rose and fell I became seven times worse. I cried out.

'"Have no fear," said my father.

'"Oh, it isn't fear, but something is coming over me which isn't right. . . ." At last I felt my belly beating against the small of my back. Then up came the burden and I threw it out.'

As the years grew on him he took an ever-increasing interest and delight in his small island world. He saw the puffins coming in from the sea with bundles of sprats across their bills, and he reflected on the ways of birds and 'what great wisdom they have to provide for their young.' At low tide when the rocks were 'warming their pates in the sun,' he watched 'the barnacles and the periwinkles loosening their hold on the stones and creeping around at their leisure.'

He tells of a whale that rose near them in their curragh. 'You could see clearly its big blue gullet which could swallow three curraghs without any trouble. We were in great danger—out in the middle of the Great Sound, a couple of miles from land, and that savage, ravenous, long-toothed monster up beside us, the way it had only to turn its head and swallow us up. I thought that at any moment we might be down in its belly.'

The day I visited the Blaskets there was neither whale to be seen nor cause for seasickness. When our curragh moved out from Dunquin, it was flat calm—the sea had a skin on it.

Through the clear water we could see the sharp teeth of submerged rocks. Gulls, white as the quartz veins in the cliffs, were soaring; choughs black as the tarred canvas of our curragh were wheeling; and a bank of mist from the sea was hiding Inishtooskert, the most northerly island of the group. We moved smoothly on a smooth sea towards the Great Blasket.

'There's only about thirty left there now,' said Kruger, the owner of our curragh. 'A couple of dozen men, four women, one child, and four cows. Half the Blaskets is gone to America. There's only been one marriage on the islands in years.'

'Small blame to them,' said Tomas who held the bow oars. 'The girls leave the island, and where would a man get a wife to go there from the mainland? No rest day or night, a woman couldn't keep going at all.'

The curraghs on the Kerry coast are similar to those of the Aran Isles but more finely cut; the bow has an easier angle, the stern a gentler sweep. But in principle of construction they are essentially the same, tarred canvas over a framework of laths. As you sit on the bottom, for there are no seats for passengers, you can feel every pulse of the Atlantic through the canvas. Because there is no keel, a rudder would be useless. Instead, each of the three rowers pulls a pair of light, narrow-bladed oars: an extra stroke on one side or the other, bow or stern, keeps the curragh on its course.

It was in this sound that, in September 1588, two ships of the Spanish Armada took refuge from the storms of the Atlantic and, having reached comparative shelter, foundered. Other ships of the same fleet were there, too, but with better fortune awaiting them. One at least reached Spain. Not so the *Santa Maria de la Rosa*, who came into the sound with her sails torn to ribbons and but one anchor, having had to slip her others when escaping from the English fire-ships. For a few hours the anchor held: then with a change of tide she began to drift. Suddenly she sank, so suddenly that every man on board was drowned save one, Antonio de Monana, who managed to reach the shore on a fragment of timber. He told of the many grandees who were on board, and mentioned that the ship contained 50,000 ducats in gold, an equal amount in silver, and a quantity of gold and silver plate. She carried '50 great pieces, all cannons of the field; 25 pieces, of brass and cast-iron belonging to the ship; there were also in her 50 tuns of sack.' Of the second ship, the *San Juan*, little is known except that she too foundered in these waters. It is thought that a small brass cannon, bearing the device of an uprooted tree, which was brought to the surface about a century ago by fishermen from the Blaskets, belonged to her.

As we came near to the Great Blasket we passed Beginish, a low flat island separated from its tall neighbour by a narrow channel.

'That was the place you 'd see the dancing in the old days,' said Kruger. 'People would be coming over from all parts of the mainland on Sunday evenings. You 'd have maybe ten or a dozen violins for the music, and they 'd dance the night away. 'Tis all finished now: 'tis like marriage—gone out of fashion.'

'Sure, there 's no one for eyther, do you see,' said Tomas.

The 'harbour' on the Great Blasket is no more than a basin in the rocks, hardly big enough for a curragh to turn, its entrance scarcely wide enough for oars to operate. The tide was low when we arrived, ribbons of oar weed were lifting and falling in the gentle swell, the wet black rocks sparkled with red anemones. We stepped ashore on to a slip, slimy with green weed, and made our way up the steep rocky slope.

Fishing-nets and lobster-pots were piled beside the track, inverted curraghs resting on their wooden supports were anchored to the ground with heavy stones. One of them, newly tarred, shone bright and smooth as patent leather.

The one village, on the sheltered landward-facing slopes of the island, is a jumble of houses and ruins of houses; among the broken walls, a maze of grass-grown paths unconsidered as rabbit tracks. Not more than an occasional chimney shows smoke; even the houses that are lived in give little sign of habitation. It is only a jersey hung out to dry, an oilskin thrown over a wall, a lobster-pot in the making outside a door, that give a hint of human tenantry. The thatch of a stone pigsty is thick with growing grass; the upturned skeleton of a curragh with the canvas rotting from its bones does duty as a hen-house.

It is the end of a community 'whose like will never be again.'

I said to a young man who was patching his boat: 'How long before *you* leave the island?'

He said: 'If the few of us that are young go away there 'll be no one to man the curraghs: the old people must be taken to the mainland, and there 's many don't want to go.'

I wandered up the grassy hill above the village towards the north side of the island, where the cliffs drop sheer into shadowed waters. It is a place of terror and foreboding even on a summer's afternoon. The history of the Great Blasket is largely a history of wrecks, of ships smashed against the buttresses of that northern shore, of ships which like those of the Armada have managed to negotiate the narrow channel into the sound, only to founder there.

On my way back I sat a while looking down over the roofs and ruins stepped one below the other on the lower slopes of the hill. Larks sang overhead, and from beyond the white beach came the sound of many cormorants rising from the sea, their feet pattering on the surface as they took off. The 'mail boat,' a curragh with three men rowing and a woman passenger in the stern, which was leaving the island as we arrived, was now almost out of sight close to the mainland. Razorbills and guillemots, singly and in skeins, were flying low over the sea. Earlier the sky had been clear; now small clouds were forming and a light breeze rippled the water.

Another islander appeared while I was making a drawing. Would I like some Kerry diamonds? he asked, pulling a handful of rock crystals out of his pocket and offering them to me. He said there were plenty of them lying about. My exchange of a quid of tobacco was as welcome to him as a packet of cigarettes had once been to a South Sea islander who offered me a handful of small pearls. In each case the tobacco had the higher financial value.

Dunlevy, for that was his name, took me to his cottage and lit a fire of shavings and small sticks to boil a kettle. He lived there with his brother, he told me—no woman in the place. The one big room was furnished with a wooden settle, a few chairs, a table, and a dresser. There was an abundance of china on the dresser, and among the plates and cups was a large recently baked bastaple loaf. A loft over each end of the room was reached by a ladder. In the one over the fireplace were stored nets, ropes, cork floats, and other fishing gear; in the other the two brothers slept. Dunlevy had no wish to leave the island: his sheep were doing well and there was a good price for wool.

The tea was hardly in the pot when Kruger came to say that the weather was changing—we ought to be going, he thought. He was followed soon after by Tomas who urged me not to delay.

The wind was certainly rising as we rowed for the shelter of Beginish. There, in the lee of the land, Kruger set a sail and soon we were leaping from crest to crest of the waves. In mid channel it was rough and spray flew from our bow, yet not a bead of water came on board. Dark clouds were gathering. An hour later, when we looked back from the top of the cliff above Dunquin harbour, the islands had vanished behind a wall of driving rain and the sound was a welter of spray.

CHAPTER TWENTY-TWO

IT WAS THE two books I have mentioned that led me to the Blaskets. It was another book that kept me staying for a week almost within sight of them. My friend Seamus Murphy had sent me a copy of his *Stone Mad*, just published, and with it an invitation to stay with him while he was on holiday in the Dingle Peninsula. My heart leapt with delight when I looked into those pages. Here was another book in the tradition of *The Islandman* and *Twenty Years a-Growing* by a man with, as he put it, 'no experience of writing and damn little schooling.' And again it was written because if he didn't make the attempt to record the way of life of 'the stonies' there was no one else to do so. 'I have often thought,' he says, 'how much knowledge drops out of our lives from one generation to the next.'

Seamus is a Cork man who after a long apprenticeship as a stonemason has become well known in Ireland as a sculptor. In his letter to me which accompanied the book he wrote: 'It is all about stone-cutters, the men that shaped me. Please tell me did I succeed in bringing them to life. I invented nothing of it—how could I?'

There was no need for Seamus to invent. He had a rich quarry of experience from which to hew his material. Listen to how he carves one facet of a fellow 'stonie':

'He was a great man to rough out a figure. He 'd put in a few lines with a bit of soft coal from the forge and then pick up a hammer-point and work away like a man in a fever. We all agreed, though, that he shouldn't be let finish a figure, because he never knew when to stop. He would have it well placed in the block, but when it came to getting in the

details he 'd go over it until it was dead.   According to the
Gospel Our Lord died when He was thirty-three, but to
judge by our man's statues, He 'd have been nearer the
pension.'

And then of a 'tramp stonie,' whose description of himself as a 'stone-cutter' created the wrong impression in the
mind of a farmer: '"Blast it," said I, "didn't we do the most
important of all jobs?   Didn't we cut the Ten Command-
ments on the slabs for Moses?   And to think that I would
live to see the day when a bostoon of a farmer would take me
for a vet!"''

When it became known in 'the yard' that a new church
was to be built in concrete: '"Isn't that nice blackguarding?
What the hell is the world coming to at all when they 're
going to build the House of God in mud?"''

In telling of work on St. Finnbarr's Cathedral he mentions
a workman who was inclined to cut the tiles on the spire
stones a bit on the rough side, and the foreman came along
and spotted it: '"It won't do, Jer," said he.   "Why?" says
me ould fella.   "Sure, 'tis going up two hundred feet an'
no one but the crows will see it."   "God will see it," says
the foreman, "an' He 's damn particular."''

From Seamus's cottage at Ballyferriter we looked north
across a wild and rocky coast, open to almost every gale from
the Atlantic.   There are few days in the year when the swell
does not break fiercely against those rocks and there is no
surge of churned up sand and foam in the bays.   When far
out to sea the white wave crests are speeding amid the flying
spume, it is said that 'Mananaan mac Lir is riding in his
chariot.'

Mananaan is in his greatest glory on nights of blackest
storm.   He is God of the Ocean: his name means 'son of the
sea': he dwells on an enchanted island, remote from other

land. His wife Fand not only excelled in beauty every queen in Ireland but was a goddess in her own right. For some reason best known to himself, Mananaan put her aside, whereupon Fand, proud and haughty, offered herself to Cuchulain, the greatest of Irish heroes. He, in spite of his wife Emer and one or two other complications, accepted the overtures, and for a time there was domestic confusion. But soon Cuchulain's love for Emer burst forth afresh and Mananaan's love for Fand was reawakened. The Druids served out a drink of forgetfulness, and all was happiness again. What a pity the secret of that drink has been lost! If the gods had need of it, how much more would a little sup of it now and again be a help to us mortals.

Looking north-east from the cottage across Smerwick Bay we could see Mount Brandon, over three thousand feet high, dominating the bare slopes of lesser hills. It was from the foot of this mountain that St. Brendan the navigator set forth on his great voyage into the Atlantic to seek the Isles of the Blest. Manuscripts dating from the seventh century narrate how, after the saint and his companions had been at sea for two days, they met Mananaan mac Lir travelling in his chariot. A conversation ensued in which the sea god explained that what appeared to the saint in his coracle as a glittering sea was to him a fertile plain:

'Where Bran sees the white of breaking waves, I see the crimson of flowers.
The fish that he sees leaping from the waters are to me young calves and lambs at play.'

This pretty fancy occurs again in the legend of St. Scuithin who could travel to Rome from Ireland in a day and thence back in another day, moving on the sea faster than if he had been on land. One day when so voyaging he met St. Finnbarr who was in a ship. 'Wherefore do you traverse the sea after this manner?' asked St. Finnbarr, to which St. Scuithin replied: 'It is not the sea on which I am travelling but a green sward rich with flowers and shamrocks.' To prove his words he bent down and gathering a wisp of blossom, threw it into the ship to St. Finnbarr. The saint from Cork, not to be outdone, stretched out his hand into the sea and drew from it a salmon which he presented to St. Scuithin. And so they went their ways having reached no conclusion.

From such light fantasies of the brain to the dry bones of history: the western extremity of the Dingle Peninsula is rich in archaeological interest. The late Professor Macalister was of opinion that nowhere in Great Britain or Ireland was there within a few acres such extensive material for the study of the early evolution of architecture. Cave dwellings, rock shelters, *clochauns* or beehive huts, prehistoric forts and Romanesque churches, all are there, including the seventh-century oratory of Gallerus, said to be the most perfect of its

period in existence. So numerous are the remains of the beehive dwellings in the Fahan district that they have been referred to as the 'ancient city of Fahan'; yet of the people who inhabited that city or their way of life nothing is known.

It would seem that the pride in dry building has persisted on the peninsula to the present day. The boundaries of mere lanes often show splendid masonry, with nothing but earth as binding material. Sometimes the construction is of small flat stones, set vertically or with the courses sloping in alternate directions, in herring-bone effect; at other times the building is cyclopean and stones worthy of a cathedral are seen in a sheep pen. I watched a mere stripling handling one of these great boulders, lifting it first on to his bent knees then getting his arms underneath and shouldering it into position.

'Ah,' he said, 'it 's a poor crow can't lift a stick.'

Ballyferriter, as the name implies, was the stronghold of the Ferriter family, the ruins of whose castle stand on a green promontory facing as wild a prospect as could threaten mariners, waves breaking on submerged reefs, jagged spires, and islands linked to each other by scarves of mist. Sea-pinks cluster about its walls and on the cliff side; yellow vetches and purple orchids match its variegated stones, while below it and around, the sea sucks and moans in gulleys and deep caverns. But of the castle only a fragment remains— 'the most of it is blown away with the years.'

Romance and tragedy have had their setting there. During the seventeenth century Pierce Ferriter, the owner of the castle, a poet and a patriot, having taken up arms against the Cromwellian forces, was obliged to leave the mainland and seek refuge on Great Blasket island. There he hid in a cave in the cliff side, 'a bed cut into the rock, the entrance no more than the height of your knee, and a little patheen to it a cat couldn't walk along.' Sheer below the 'patheen' was a cavern, in and out of which the ocean surged. One night when visiting a cottage not far from his hiding place, Ferriter found himself surrounded by troops. It seemed that there could be no escape. He suggested, however, to the woman of the house that she should prepare food for the soldiers and, being like her an Irish speaker, he was also able to suggest that whenever she was passing the rifles which were leaning, muzzles up, against the walls, she should let a few drops of water slide into the barrels. Next morning the soldiers with their prisoner set out for the landing place, taking a short cut over the hill which their hostess had indicated. Nearing his den, Ferriter broke from his guard and ran. Every gun was levelled at him and every gun failed to fire. Inside the entrance to his cave, Ferriter awaited his captors. They could approach only in single file. As each one bent low to come through the entrance, 'he met a clout of a stick on the head which sent him sprawling into the water below.' Not one of the armed party survived the day. Neither, in fact, did Ferriter himself survive long afterwards, for, having been taken prisoner on the mainland, he was hanged in Killarney along with a bishop and a priest.

It was an ancestor of his, another Pierce Ferriter, who persuaded Sybil, the daughter of Roderick Lynch, a chieftain of Galway, to elope with him almost from under the nose of a prince of Ulster to whom her father had promised her in marriage. Pursued by the father as well as by the prince and his retainers, Ferriter hid his lady in a cave, this time in the cliff under the castle, while he went forth to do battle. Having slain the prince in single combat and made peace with the father, he returned only to find that in his absence a tidal wave had swept into the cave and drowned his bride. Sybil Head, the high promontory overlooking Ferriter's Castle, takes its name from the unfortunate heroine.

Yet a third Pierce Ferriter at a later date sailed into Galway Bay and abducted the daughter of the chieftain O'Luinn. This time the conclusion was a happier one, for 'if the man from Galway sent ships to blast the castle, didn't Pierce use persuasion, and soon there was banks of love between them all.'

A few miles to the north of Ballyferriter, across the wide saucer of marshland where in summer small black cattle graze loin-deep in golden iris and the hedges are creamed with honeysuckle, lies Smerwick Bay. There, in the year 1580, occurred one of those acts of barbarism which so often are committed in the name of religion or culture.

Queen Elizabeth was at that time endeavouring to suppress the Roman Catholic religion in Ireland, and a small force of men, Italian and Spanish, had come to join the Irish in their struggle for the older faith. This force was encamped at Dunanoir in Smerwick Harbour and Elizabeth's deputy, Earl Grey, laid siege to them. Here are his words describing to her the surrender of the garrison on the morning of the 10th November:

'The Colonel came forth with ten or twelve of his chief gentlemen, trailing their ensigns rolled up, and presented them to me with their lives and the Fort. I sent straight, certain gentlemen in, to see their weapons and armour laid down, and to guard the munition and victual, there left, from spoil. Then put I in certain bands who straight fell to execution. There were six hundred slain.'

In her official reply the queen refers to this enterprise as 'greatly to her liking' and adds a foreword in her own writing: 'The mighty hand of the Almightiest power hath showed manifest the force of His strength in the weakness of feeblest sex, and minds this year to make men ashamed ever hereafter to disdain us. In which action I joy that you have been chosen the instrument of His glory, which I mean to give you no cause to forthink. Your loving Sovereign, Elizabeth R.'

Two years later, by which time grim details not mentioned in Grey's first letter must have come to her notice, she writes to him that she could never forget his 'great good services' especially the 'exploit you did against the strangers that had invaded the realm.'

From the low-lying dunes on the western side of Smerwick Bay the land flows gently towards the Atlantic until, as it nears the coast, it rises suddenly into three high, wave-like crests that tower above the ocean. It is as though land and sea had reversed their roles. Many a ship has met her fate on the rocks below: many a cottager living on those sparse hills has been thankful for what the ocean has cast ashore.

In a sheltered gulley not far from the cliffs, I saw the water cloudy with delicate filamentous beings. Flashes of light shot through the fluorescent mass. Thousands of separate entities were pulsating in that narrow stretch of water. Some no bigger than a gooseberry were like Chinese lanterns of translucent silk, others were bell-shaped fringed with fine beaded threads to guard the petalled flower within. Some were like miniature cups, others resembled saucers, gently undulating or momentarily floating inert. Small jelly-fish like smoke rings sailed among them as moons among their satellites, and below all moved a tangle of brown weed whose fronds were broad as tropic leaves, whose texture was close woven as untrodden jungle.

Seamus and I went shopping in Ballyferriter. We chose a packet of dried peas, and then we dropped into John Long's bar. We were discussing the peculiarities of various stones for carving, and I mentioned a friend of mine who had been commissioned to carve a Venus in Hopton Wood stone. Unfortunately the piece chosen for the job held a fragment of shell which duly appeared in the shape and in the position of an appendix scar. Nothing could be done to remove it, and the deeper the sculptor cut into the stone the longer grew the scar. Seamus said that at Ballinsloe in County Galway he had seen two ewers cut from the local stone. 'Their walls were as thin as those of bedroom jugs: 'twas a miracle the way the handles were relieved. You couldn't do a job of that kind if there was a flaw in the stone. And there wasn't a trace of a tool mark inside or out.'

Somehow or other our conversation came round to the massacre at Smerwick. Gerald Sayers, who was serving us, a powerful man with the high forehead and finely chiselled features that one often meets in Kerry, bent down and picked up from behind the counter a cannon ball. 'Thirteen pounds seven ounces it weighs,' he said. 'They came on it ten feet down in a bog. There's a lot of them found about the place. There's skulls and bones, too,' he added, 'all along the coast, from the massacre. The sea opens up the graves and the bones come out. Did you know young O'Driscoll?' he asked.

'I knew of him,' said Seamus

'He's doing atom bombs now,' said Sayers. 'They say he's a wonder for the science. He used to be in here many a time. He said it took him six glasses of whiskey to pass his matric. The first time he went in he was cold sober and he failed. The second time he went in he couldn't see the paper he was writing on, and he passed with honours. Now he has all the degrees in the world. He must have a fine open brain.'

Our host left us for a moment while he went next door to buy a packet of cigarettes. He said that just now he was building, and that required a great concentration of thought; a pipe was no good to him when he was thinking, but a cigarette cleared his brain. When he came back he climbed on to a small triangular ledge set in the angle between the porch and the counter. With a foot on either of two barrels and his back into the corner, he lit a cigarette.

'Me and Johnny O'Driscoll was at school at the same time,' he said, 'and 'twas one day he brought in with him a skull he'd found on the shore. And when the master was out didn't he stick a cap on the skull's head and a clay pipe in between his teeth, and he left it there on the master's bench. I tell you 'twas murder when the master came in. The priest was called and they nearly skelped the life out of poor Johnny. "Take it back with you," they said, "to where you found it." Sure the first furze bush Johnny met, didn't he throw the skull in under it and away with him.'

From cannon balls we went on to discuss the respective merits of the differing games of football: Rugby which is 'mostly played by the referee on his whistle,' soccer where "'tis like a railway junction with fellows shunting in to you,' and Gaelic where all personal assault is against the rules and bouncing, punching, and kicking the ball combine to make a game that is nearly as fast as hurling, which, after all, is nearly as fast as polo. I suggested that hurling beat them all for roughness, with the sticks swung left and swung right high above the shoulder, and the ball in the air more often than not.

"'Tis only ignorance makes it rough,' said Seamus. 'If you know what your man may do, you'll know how to circumvent him.'

'Isn't that the way of life?' said Gerald.

CHAPTER TWENTY-THREE

TWO MONTHS AFTER the shearing in June, 'the boys' at Gougane had collected for the dipping. Again they were out on the hills at dawn, and again the sheep from the northern mountain were rounded up and brought down to the pen. The large concrete pit into which earlier in the year the shorn fleeces had been thrown was now filled with liquid, and into this every animal had to go. It was dropped tail first, so that for a moment it was totally immersed, and then guided here and there with a crook until the minute glass had run its course.

Now the hills were heather tinted, and velvet-winged peacock butterflies fluttered from bell to bell. The men in skin-tight jerseys worked among unkempt ewes and rams. Dappled light fell on bedraggled fleeces.

A newcomer, Paddy Brady from near Kilgarvan, joined the ranks. He told me how some poachers had been getting fish in his district. A few handfuls of gravel with oil poured over them, he said, is how they clear the water. The stones are thrown high into the air so that they scatter over the pool; then when they strike the water the oil leaves them, and the poachers can see if there's a fish there. If there is, they send a terrier into the pool and keep him splashing about until the fish gets frightened and hides under the bank. Then a gaff or a stroke-haul does the rest.

On his way to Gougane, Paddy had travelled a bit of the way with some tinkers. They had a girl up for marriage, and were giving £300 with her. There had been some slight altercation with the police a few miles back. '"What's

your address?" asked the guards. "Under the rising sun,"
said the tinker.'

Paddy was only out of hospital a few days, and wasn't able
to do much work, so he had plenty of time for talk. They
thought he 'd had an ulcer, he told me, and that they 'd have
to operate, but they hadn't done it in the end. 'Well,' he
said, 'I never put down such a day in me life as that day I
went in. I was in Cork before noon, and 'twasn't till six
o'clock in the evening that I could face up to it. The wife
took me to the pictures, and what was it but them fellows
dying in the snow. "For the love of God, come out of
this," I said. So then we went to get a cup of tea, and I
couldn't drink it—'twas that weak 'twas like water.
"We 'll go for a walk down the Mardyke and have a look at
the river," says me wife. Would you believe it, before we
got to the first seat it was raining. So at six o'clock she left
me at the gate, and who did I meet coming out but Paddy
Byrne. "What ails you?" he says. "An ulcer," I told
him. "Oh, my God," he said, "there 's poor Jackie Shea
inside and he after being operated on for the same thing, and
he 'll never recover."'

'You thought your axle was broke that time,' said Michael.

'I tell you,' said Pat, 'if a nurse hadn't caught a hold of me
at that moment, I 'd have bolted like a rabbit. "Go through
the door at the end there," she says, "and they 'll look after
you." Well, I could hardly walk with the fear that was on
me. Me own sweat was tripping me. "Get into bed
now," says another nurse. "I 'll put the screens around you
while you undress," she said. And in all the beds around me
there wasn't a face that I knew. I sat down on the bed to
take off me boots—they 'll never go on me again, I thought,
I wonder who 'll wear them after I 'm gone. And the new
pants on me, too. 'Twould have been better maybe if I 'd

come in in the old ones, maybe the family would never get them back. And when I undid me collar the button came off. Small matter, I thought.

'And then, while I was bending down, didn't a voice say over the screen: "How 's yourself, Pat?" And when I looked up, wasn't it Tom Cooney from Ardtully. Well, 'twas as if I 'd hooked a two-pound trout. "Yerra, man, 'tis grand in here," says he. "Jack Keogh is after going out yesterday, loose as a hare, and I 'll be going out meself next week." Before I was five minutes in bed the nurse was in with a trayful of tea, and sure from that on I was like a horse in his own stable.'

The work continued. Dan Borlin was lifting full-grown sheep as if they were lambs. 'You must hold them by the wool on their belly or you 'll hurt them,' he said. Timmy Leary was guiding them gently through the dip. Regularly, the hatch of iron sheeting was lifted to let the drenched animals scramble under it to a solid footing.

Teigue the Pass, with a joke in his eye as usual, came up the hill. 'Will any of ye be going to the circus to-night?' he asked.

'I dunno is it any good,' said Con Borlin.

'They 're paying a shilling a head for rabbits to feed the lions,' said Teigue. 'There won't be a rabbit left in the country after they 're gone. And they 're netting all the lakes for pike for the water-lion—he takes a ton of fish a day. And the clowns is wonderful, lepping about on telegraph wires across the hall.'

'Go on away out of that with your stories,' said Michael Kelly. ''Tis no more than talkies is there. "Lyons Talkies"—that 's what there is.'

Teigue was laughing.

'I never seen one of them in me life,' said Con.

'Yerra, man, they 're grand. There was a fellow there last night and he up on a white horse. My God! You never seen such riding. Himself and his crowd was after some fellows had stolen their cattle. Shooting and banging they were, roaring up and down hills—there was a girl with them, too—you 'd think the horses would be destroyed: they 'd never do it in this country, they 'd be bogged.'

'I seen a film once about Killarney,' said Paddy. ''Twas about a fellow drowning a girl in the lake. 'Twould make you laugh, man, to see the sheep—they don't grow that high in Killarney, nor so big in the bone. There wasn't one of them would live on the mountain.'

The last few sheep came through the dip. Paddy picked up a long-handled sieve and began to clear the surface of the liquid of its accumulated dirt. Jer took a brush and swept the animals' droppings from the floor of the pen. The dogs woke up and were on their feet, eager to be away with the men to gather another batch of sheep from the southern mountain.

I struck eastwards along the hill-side, to find Batty Kit putting thatch on a clamp of turf. He stopped work as I came towards him.

'I 'm destroyed with the stiffness,' he said, rubbing his hip.

'What brought it on?' I asked.

'Begor, I suppose 'twas the lifting of the big stones when I was a little boy that softened the bones in me. They 're gone stiff on me now,' he said. 'The big rocks was heavy for a boy.'

'But you 're grand for your age,' I said.

'Thanks be to God I am, but sure eighty-two isn't so much after all.'

Batt had started work when he was eleven years old. His father died young, leaving a widow and seven children, and times were bad. They lived in a cabin on the mountainside, and their food was for the most part potatoes and yellow meal with now and again 'a few groceries' after the mother had been to market. She used to leave the house at two o'clock in the morning and walk the twenty-one miles to Dunmanway, taking with her the few pounds of butter she had made. When she had sold these, she would buy what she could afford in the way of tea and sugar, and then walk the twenty-one miles home, getting there before dusk. She had to be back before dusk as she was doing the milking for a farmer on the other side of the valley. 'It wouldn't do to keep waiting the cows.' Batt was paid five shillings a week when he started work, his job being to help with the clearing of the stones in Keimaneigh Pass. ''Twas no more than a track in them days. You could ride a horse through it but you couldn't take a cart.' He continued at that work for nine years, getting eight shillings a week as he became more skilled. Then he went to work for a farmer where his wages were four pounds ten a year with his keep. It was there that he had his first taste of bread. 'Well!' he said, 'when I ate a couple of slices of the bread I felt that light I could have jumped over the house.' That, however, wasn't the end of his troubles, for the potato crop failed next year, and he was

glad to make a meal of the skins left over from the farmer's dinner.

When Batty was first employed on the roads he went barefoot. It wasn't until he had worked for several months that he had saved enough money to buy himself a pair of boots. His mother then, barefoot herself, walked the twenty miles to Macroom and back again to get him what he needed. Owing to bad weather she had to shelter overnight on her way back, and it wasn't till the next morning when Batt was on his way to work that she met him, this side of the crossroads, just by the little bridge over the stream that flows down from the pass.

'"Put 'em on you now," she said. So begod, I sat down,' said Batty, 'on the wall of the little bridgeen, and I drew on the boots. Faith, I thought I was the grandest man that ever walked the roads that morning. But begod, 'twas on that same little bridgeen that I sat down, coming home at nightfall, to draw off the boots. They had the toes pinched on me. I tell you, it wasn't till I'd walked through the bogs in them that I could wear them without the pinch.

It took the water, do you see, to soften the leather, to shape
it, you might say, to the foot. I tell you, now, if ever you
have a new pair of boots and they pinches you, go and stand
in a stream or in a pool of water in the bog, and let the water
fill the boots, and then walk them till they be dry on your
feet, and ever after they 'll fit you like wool.'

From where we were sitting beside the turf clamp we
could see the roof of Batty's cottage.

'They made a good job with the slates for you,' I said.

'And wasn't it right for them, too?' said Batt. 'Wasn't
it a fierce blast of powder they put in? Sure, the stones were
coming through the sky like crows. 'Twas by the will of
God no one was hurt.'

Earlier in the year, men widening the road from Gougane
had found it necessary to blast a rock immediately in front of
Batt's cottage and, whatever the reason, the explosion had
been more violent than was expected. Boulders had been
blown into Batt's garden; everything growing there had been
destroyed. The blast had split the wall of the shed adjoining
his cottage and large stones dropping through the roof of his
house had created havoc within. 'Thanks be to God the pig
in the shed wasn't hurt!' said Batt.

Sitting there on the bank of turf, Batt told me of his sister
Elly who in those early days of which I have spoken had gone
to work for a farmer in Kerry.

'She 'd be earning maybe three or four pounds a year and
her keep,' he said, 'and the farmer's wife was that mean and
hard she hid the girl's comb so she wouldn't be spending a
morsel of time on her hair.'

In harvest time Elly was expected to help in the fields after
she had finished her work in the house, and one of her jobs
there was to bind into sheaves the corn that had been cut
during the day. It didn't matter how much lay there, she

had to gather and bind it, if she stayed out till midnight. 'They showed no mercy on her at all,' said Batt. And one day, after she 'd been kept in the house till past four o'clock, she went out and when she got into the field didn't she find an extra reaper had been there and more than ever was waiting for her. And she knew she 'd never get it done, and she was tired, and sadness came on her and she sat down and cried. And after she had cried for a bit she began to pray, and she prayed that her father who was dead would come and help her. 'On my soul,' said Batty, 'within one quarter of an hour every blade of that corn that was lying in the field was gathered and bound.'

CHAPTER TWENTY-FOUR

THE AFTERNOON WAS FINE when I set out to find the source of the River Blackwater on the slopes of Knock-anefune, over the Kerry border. The scent of meadow-sweet was heavy in the air, and I thought of those lines in Ethel Rolt-Wheeler's poem:

> 'Meadow-sweet and meadow-sweet
>   All the way to Tara;
> Shrill of whispers in the wheat,
> Bees that hum and lambs that bleat . . .
> Ghosts that wear a winding-sheet . . .
>   This is Royal Tara;
> Hosts of ghosts the meadow-sweet
>   All the way to Tara.'

Tara, the throne of kings from prehistoric times to the sixth century; Tara where, if tradition is to be believed, the first law of copyright was formulated.

During the reign of Dermot son of Fergus, King of Ireland 544–65, St. Columkille, Abbot of Iona, paid a visit to St. Finian of Movilla in Ulster, and while there he borrowed from his host a book of psalms which he greatly admired. Fearful of refusal if he asked permission to make a copy of it, he transcribed the pages secretly. St. Finian discovering this claimed the copy as his own because, he said, it had been made from his book and without his consent. There followed then a very worldly dispute between the two holy men as to the ownership of those pages, until eventually they agreed to lay their case before the king at Tara. Dermot, having heard the evidence, pronounced judgment: 'The calf, being the offspring of the cow, belongeth to the cow: so the copy, being the offspring of the book, belongeth to the book.' He thus awarded the copy to St. Finian; but it is nice to know that, soon after the decision, the copy was given back to St. Columkille whose kindred, the O'Donnells, treasured it for many generations. It became their *Cathach*, their 'battler,' a sacred relic to be borne, sun-wise, three times round their army before battle to ensure victory, and was so used by them as late as the fifteenth century. To-day the elaborate case in which it was carried, of silver gilt, enamel, and precious stones, may be seen in the National Museum, Dublin.

My road over the mountains led me into ever-narrowing lanes until finally I stopped the car at the mouth of a bhoreen. Ahead of me the first trickle of the Blackwater was 'twisting and turning like a wor-rum' through a gentle fertile valley. Here the river forms the county bounds, and the stream is so narrow that cattle grazing in Kerry can, if they so wish, change to pasturage in County Cork without as much as wetting their feet.

It was a Kerry man who said to me: 'How could you possibly write a book about a little local stream like the Lee when you have the noble Blackwater, "the Irish Rhine," that rises in Kerry, there before you?'

'Well,' I said, 'the Blackwater may rise in Kerry but it gets out of it and into Cork at the first opportunity. It is only in Cork that it achieves the full majesty of its flow.'

There has always been a friendly rivalry between the two neighbouring counties. The story goes that a young man unable to make a living on a sparse mountainside in Kerry went east to Mallow in County Cork, where the land is rich, to work for a farmer. 'It was harvest time and it was a wonderful harvest; you could hardly count the cocks they had, and they were binding them up with sugauns (straw ropes). "Well, Kerryman," said the farmer, "I suppose you never seen the like of this with your eyes before." "I am surprised at a man like you expressing yourself like that," said the Kerry man. "The sop you have in this hag-gard wouldn't make sugauns for my ricks."'

And if Kerry men are proud, the Kerry women are modest. The town of Abbeyfeale derives its name from this virtue. 'At one time there was no town there at all, only the river, and one day a woman by the name of Fial went bathing herself. She was the wife of some sort of chieftain, and 'twas a day in the middle of June, and when she came out of the water she stood in her pelt in the sun to dry herself. And while she was standing there, didn't she see a man in the distance looking at her. With that she dropped dead on the spot with shame—I dunno would a girl do it to-day—and who was the man after all but her husband. So, anyway, they called the river after her, and in the years that followed the monks came and built an abbey alongside of it, and that 's how Abbeyfeale got the name.'

Below me tiny rapids were babbling between dry beaches of shingle and I was preparing to follow their course on foot, upwards, through the gorse and iris and spurge that lined their banks, when I noticed that one of the tyres of my van was flat. That meant a delay—more than a delay, for the slope and the surface of the road made it impossible to use the jack single-handed. A mist had begun to fall.

Behind the near hill I could see the smoke from a cottage. Maybe there was someone there who could help.

'Wouldn't you come in out of the wet and have a cup of tea?' said the young woman who answered my knock. 'The kettle is boiling and himself will be in directly.'

An old woman was sitting by the fire, tying a bundle of turkey quills into a brush for the hearth. Without moving from her chair she shook hands and welcomed me. The kettle was on the crane and the teapot was standing among some

glowing fragments of turf at the edge of the fire. Although the floor of the room was of cement and cobbles the fire was built on bare protruding rock. The room was furnished with an old oak settle with panelled back, a table, a few chairs, and a small cupboard that held oddments of china. A staircase at the far end led to an upstairs room; a door at the back of the room opened on to stone steps set into the side of the hill. Through it I could see hens and guinea-fowl picking in the grass, almost at ceiling level.

'Shut one of them doors, Bridie,' said the old lady. In Kerry it is thought unlucky to have front and back door open at the same time, as it is also thought unlucky to go out by a different door to the one by which you entered.

There came the sound of heavy boots on the paving-stones outside and the man of the house came in. He hung a horse collar and a whip over the head of the stair rail and came towards me.

'This is my husband,' said Bridie.

'You 're welcome,' he said, shaking hands. He was about thirty years of age, splendidly built, with a powerful neck set on massive shoulders.

'It 's a soft evening,' I said.

'Good for the growth,' he said.

Bridie put some eggs to boil in a tin among the turfs.

'Is it yours the van is below?' asked the husband.

'It is,' I said, 'and there 's a nail in the tyre.'

'That 's poor employment for a nail,' he said.

'Maybe 'tis better there than in the sole of his foot,' said Bridie.

'Wouldn't Jerry fix that for him, Dan?' asked the mother.

'We 'll have to lift the car,' I said. 'The jack is no use.'

'Jerry would lift the six foot of earth off the lid of his own coffin,' said Dan.

'Is he far away?' I inquired.

''Tis only two throws of a bowl before you from the cross. Slip down, Bridie, and tell him come up,' said Dan.

'Draw up and take your tea,' said Bridie, lifting the eggs out of the tin and putting them with the teapot on the table.

She went out of the door and I, also, did as I was told. Dan sat up to the table too, but the old woman stayed by the fire.

''Twas you I seen at the City on May Day,' said Dan.

'It probably was,' I said.

''Tis nothing like the old days now,' he said. 'When I was a boy you couldn't move with the crowd.'

'When I was a girl you couldn't get there with the people in squadrons on the road,' said his mother.

'And I seen you again in Kilnacrom, the Monday of the fight.'

'I missed that,' I said.

'You passed through early. 'Twas a real faction fight. There hasn't been the like for years. 'Twas some bit of old spite. Two fellows started and all the cousins and second cousins and thirty-first cousins joined in. There was twenty men a side fighting, the real old style with sticks—cut, thrust, and parry as if they had been swords.'

'Well, isn't it a grand thing,' said his mother, 'to see the old spirit again. With them holy and blessed fights in the old days, the world was very quiet.'

'A kettle that boils over often cleans the hearth,' said Dan. 'They tell me,' he added, 'there isn't a town in the world you haven't put your foot.'

'There's plenty of them,' I said.

'And I suppose the Irish is everywhere.'

'Everywhere,' I said, 'and often in trouble.'

Then I told them of 'Tom the Divil,' an Irishman who during the last century reached eminence in Samoa. Whether he was a runaway sailor or an escaped convict nobody was quite sure, but he soon achieved great influence and power on Manono and, like myself, was created a high chief of that island. Unlike myself, however, he was a great fighter and in the many local wars became the terror of the enemy. Again unlike myself, any girl he fancied was given to him immediately. When I mentioned this, Dan's eyes sparkled. His mother, still by the fire, murmured 'Oh, oh, oh!'

Eventually, despite his rank—and mine—Tom's conduct became unbearable. Even his friends felt unsafe in his presence, for he liked nothing better than a fight on the village green. One evening while a number of girls engaged his attention, four young men with clubs stole upon him, and the clubs met simultaneously on his head. His last words were: 'My club! My club!'

'Didn't he have great spirit after all,' said Dan. His mother by the fire said nothing, but sighed deeply.

By this Dan and I had finished our tea, and Bridie had come back. Wouldn't I like a few more eggs? she asked.

'Pull up your chair,' said Dan, moving towards the hearth. 'A fire is a good comrade a night like this.'

'God save all here,' said a man, looking in over the half-door.

'And you too,' said Dan and his mother.

'The van's outside,' he said.

'Is it fixed, Jerry?' asked Dan.

'I put on the spare wheel,' said Jerry.

'Wouldn't you sit down a while,' said Dan. He pulled forward a chair for Jerry and then went out through the back door.

'Tell me,' I whispered to Jerry, 'how much do I owe you?'

'Yerra, don't be talking!' he replied.

Dan came back with a bottle in his hands. Bridie filled a small jug with water from a large bucket. There was no mistaking the bouquet when the cork was drawn. There was no mistaking the smoothness to the tongue when the glass was filled, or the fire in one's belly when the glass was emptied.

As Jerry said: 'Don't be talking!' You never seen the like of the dancing that happened that night. The boys came in and the girls came in. They began with puss-music and they finished up with three fiddles. They sang in Irish and they sang in English, and at the end of every verse, or nearly every verse, there were cries of 'Good boy!' or 'Good girl!' 'Good! Lovely, lovely!' just as in Samoa they would call '*Malie, malie!*' meaning 'Beautiful!' If there was a pause in the music, it was only while our glasses were being refilled or while more food was put on the table. Dan sat beside me in merry mood. His mother, still by the fire, was smiling. Bridie's eyes were flashing and her hair was flying as she swung with the music. She and Dan had only been married a few months. There was no weight of children on them yet.

CHAPTER TWENTY-FIVE

UNLIKE THE LEE, which flows 'unsullied by a town,' the Blackwater has many accretions of buildings on its banks.

> 'Mallow, Mallow, Cappoquin,
> Doneraile, Charleville;
> Broken windows upside down,
> Hey! for the rakes of Mallow town.'

Although during the greater part of the eighteenth century the warm springs of Mallow had 'great repute for cleansing the stomach and *primae viae*, correcting the peccant humours lodged there, and opening the obstructed glands,' it seems that many visitors to the spa paid more attention to the curative powers of claret and whiskey. At that time the town owed much of its prosperity to the influx of visitors who sought a cure or incurred the need for one. Being also the centre of a racing and hunting country there was no shortage of gaiety. Though the rakes were probably as stupid and useless as any other coterie of the kind, they spent money, and money often purchases forgiveness. The town is still a centre for hunting and fishing, but 'blackguarding' is no longer fashionable. Prosperity comes through more reasonable channels. The rakehells have gone their way.

From Mallow to the sea there are nearly sixty miles of ever-varying stream: gentle scaurs among lush meadows, calm stretches reflecting beech and oak woods, dark pools under overhanging limestone cliffs, sudden vistas of distant hills, ruined castles in abundance. The river is best seen from on foot along its banks. You can travel for miles along the road that winds beside it and see nothing to entrance you but stone walls. The land is rich, probably as rich as anywhere in Ireland or Great Britain, and those who at the time of the confiscations accepted these estates coffined themselves within such barricades, twelve or even fifteen feet high.

Strictly speaking, Doneraile is on a tributary of the Blackwater, the Awbeg, Spenser's 'Mulla mine.' In March 1854, on the night of the death of the third Viscount Doneraile, a farmer on the road late at night met a coach drawn by four headless horses. It was preceded by a huge yellow hound and followed by another. In August 1887, when the fourth Viscount died, a farmer passing Doneraile on his way to Mallow saw a similar apparition, and yet again at a later date, when another of the family died, the same was seen. There is no dearth of other strange happenings in the district. A lady in white climbs over a high wall at dusk to visit the spot where centuries ago her lover was killed. A boy 'all burning over with stars' appears sitting on the top of an old gate and threatens to throw a fiery missile at passers-by. On the road between Ballyandrew and Doneraile Park a skeleton may be seen running along the road holding in his hand a ball of yellow light. There are stories of ghostly huntsmen and hounds, and of two nuns who appear at midnight at the holy well in Drenagh wood.

Charleville, twelve miles to the north of Doneraile, is close to that outworn seat, Gibbings Grove. Here, according to Smith's *History of Cork*, was found 'in the centre of a large stone, the rowel of a spur,' a fact which seemed to the historian to be 'an evident proof of the growth of stones.' For myself, I incline to the idea that the find was a relic of the Bronze Age, a mould from which for some reason the casting had not been removed.

For me the Blackwater is associated chiefly with the town

of Fermoy which sits astride its banks some fifteen miles east
of Mallow.   There I went to my first boarding school, at the
age of eleven, and there I experienced my first pangs of
loneliness.   I liked the headmaster and I admired his wife.
She had a baby during my first term, a complete surprise to
me, though some of the senior boys said that of course they
knew.   This business of babies was very mystifying to me
just then.   Twice it had occurred in my own family without
apparently a word of warning.   It just happened.   I had gone
to bed as usual the night before, and next morning there was
my mother with a baby in her arms.   After the second of
these events, I determined that I would keep a very close
watch, and I did so for several months without any results.
Then the idea went out of my head.   And now at Fermoy
almost the very same thing had occurred again!

At that school I first learned of compulsory games.   Till
I went there I thought games were pastimes to be enjoyed
when one felt like playing; I hadn't realized that they were
more important than classroom study.   And it took me a
long while to understand why, having run all over the field
till I hadn't a breath left in my body, I should get a furious
kick in my bottom from a husky full-back, twice my size,
with the injunction, 'Play up!'   I was never built for such
violent and continued exertion, but I shone at the end of a
tug-of-war rope where my instructions were 'Lie on it!'

When my father moved to Carrigrohane, a parish within a
few miles of Cork, I went to a day school in the city.   The
headmaster, a clergyman, wore rubber-soled shoes and had
glass fitted in the doors of all the rooms.   In his class school
began each day with gabbled prayers, the prayer merging
without a pause into the subject of the first hour's teaching:
' . . . through Jesus Christ our Lord Amen $x^2 + y^2 +$ some-
thing-or-other equals what?   Hands up when you 've got it.

Come on, get on your seats quickly!' I learned nothing there except the answers to a few questions that enabled me to pass matric.

A few miles from Fermoy, on the Mallow side, is Bally-hooly, *Baile-atha-ubhla*, 'the town of the ford of the apple.' When in the seventh century St. Mochuda, Bishop of Lismore, on his travels came to the site of this town he found at the ford an apple floating in the river. The chief of the district was waiting to receive him, and with him was his daughter whose right arm was paralysed. Mochuda offered her the apple. The child put out her left hand to take it. 'No,' he said, 'take it with your right.' And straightway putting out her right hand she took the apple and was healed —a form of treatment by suggestion not unknown to doctors to-day.

Not quite so easy to believe is the story of a girl who, under a spell cast by her jealous sister, lives in a cave under Castle Cor near Fermoy. Seated on a throne, in the form of a white cat, she guards vast treasures of silver and gold. For one week each year, at midsummer, she is able to resume her human shape, and if any one seeing her then should love her for herself alone and not for the jewels, the spell will be broken. But 'who the hell could get through the door of that cave where a ferret wouldn't fit?'

Much of the history of the lower reaches of the Blackwater consists of sad accounts of risings and subsequent beheadings and hangings in chains. Tragedy and treachery filled the valley as surely as the peace that flows between the river's banks to-day. And there were the same conflicts between high ideals and human weaknesses that must ever be. Queen Elizabeth sent presents in the shape of gowns worn by her royal self to the wives of insurgent chiefs, such as Turlough O'Neill in Ulster, and Garret, Earl of Desmond, in

Munster, hoping to win them over. Even though these garments were 'slobbered in the front breadth' and had to be repaired with new materials before presentation, we learn that after this 'the Countess of Desmond greatly disapproved of her husband's disloyal conduct.' Her gown was of cloth of gold.

From Dromana Castle near the mouth of the river at Youghal, where the old Countess of Desmond lived to the age of 104, 140, or 162 according to varying reports and only died after falling from a cherry-tree into which she had climbed for the fruit, there comes the strange history of the marriage of Catherine Fitzgerald. In May 1673 in Lambeth Chapel, Gilbert Sheldon, then Archbishop of Canterbury, sealed in holy wedlock this heiress aged twelve, and John De la Poer, not yet eight years old. Catherine 'by deed of feoffment' had been left large estates, and her guardians, relatives of the bridegroom, were anxious to secure the property for their family. Unfortunately for them, Catherine, even as a child, had strong views about her person, and on Easter Eve 1676 she eloped with Edward Villiers, a Cornet of Horse, son of Viscount Grandison. The fat was in the fire, and we find Robert Power, a lawyer of Lincoln's Inn, writing of this child that he does not 'present unto her objects of terror, to frighten her with guilty apprehensions, or to tax her with the polluted mystery of a matrimonial bed, or the stain of unchaste extravagancies, or to convene her before the Great Judge of Heaven and Earth, who is so formidable to the sense of guilt; or to upbraid her with the inevitable consequences of her ruin,' etc. Long litigation followed, with many appeals, until eventually Catherine became legally Mrs. Villiers. She and her husband were welcomed at court, after which he was promoted to lieutenant-colonel of the first troop of Horse Guards, and later to brigadier-general. He died in 1693, and a few years later she consoled herself with a lieutenant-general.

The histories of Lismore and Youghal would each need a volume to itself. *Lis mor*, meaning 'the great fort,' was at one time the chief seat of learning in Ireland, whither

came scholars from all parts of Britain and Europe, including, it is said, King Alfred of England. There are some who aver that it was while at Lismore that the king acquired that skill on the Irish harp which enabled him later to disguise himself as a harper and so gain admission to the tent of Guthrum, Prince of Denmark. Whether this is history or romance it is hard to determine, but we do know from a contemporary of his that the king sought knowledge from beyond the confines of his own kingdom. Bishop Asser of St. David's wrote of him: 'As the most prudent bee, rising early on a summer morning from its busy hive, directing its course in swift flight through the uncertain paths of the air, descends upon the manifold and varied flowers of herbs, grasses, and shrubs, and chooses what pleases it most, and so carries it home, thus did the king direct the eyes of his mind to a distance, and seek from without what he did not possess close at hand, within his own kingdom.'

From the time of Henry II until the reign of Elizabeth the territory from Youghal, at the mouth of the river, in the east, to Tralee in the west belonged to the Geraldines, Earls of Desmond, of whom Macaulay wrote that 'they were the greatest and proudest subjects that any Sovereign of Europe ever had.' In the reign of Edward IV by the treachery of the queen they were driven into open rebellion. In the reign of Elizabeth, Garret, the sixteenth and last regnant earl, was killed by the treachery of one of his own people, and his head sent to London as a present to the queen. A later namesake of his, after his castle at Templemichael, near Youghal, had been reduced by Cromwell, retired, without surrendering, to one of his remaining estates on the other side of the river. There in due course he died and was buried. But on the night after his burial, and for several years to come on its anniversary, there was heard at Templemichael from across the river a wailing cry: '*Garralth harroing! Garralth harroing!*' meaning 'Give Garret a ferry!' Eventually some of the men from Templemichael crossed the river, exhumed the body, and bringing it back with them buried it in the graveyard beside the castle. Since then 'the last of the Geraldines' has slept in peace.

CHAPTER TWENTY-SIX

BY ROYAL PROCLAMATION
PUCK FAIR
Killorglin
10, 11, 12 August, 1949
Ireland's Oldest and Largest Horse, Cattle, Sheep & Pig Fair

Don't fail to see the enthronement of
IRELAND'S ONLY KING
OF THE FAIR—one of the few remaining
Monarchs who, under Royal Constitution
'as old as time,' rules beyond party or
treaty a Kingdom and a People catering
during the Carnival for the business and
the pleasure of the multitude, and inviting
all and sundry to partake of the happy and
enjoyable atmosphere of a carefree realm.

So read the poster. For twenty miles outside the town, on the first day, known as 'gathering day,' I passed droves of cattle, a dozen here, a dozen there, an occasional herd of perhaps thirty or forty; some black, some roan, some red. Ponies and horses were on the road, too, led or driven, chestnuts and greys and piebalds; and flocks of sheep, horned and hornless; and pigs, old and young, in cribs on horse or donkey carts. And then for a quarter of a mile along the road that leads from north and south to the bridge across the River Laune, the gateway to the town, there was a gipsy encampment. Caravan after caravan, each one rich in bright paint, rich in bright brass, rich in carved timbers.

Inside and outside these barrel-shaped dwellings are strong-featured women, some with hair red as copper, others with hair black as kettles. They wear brightly coloured dresses, canary yellow, scarlet, magenta. The walls of the caravans are panelled with gay cottons or chintzes and, as if to make the cramped space inside more cramped, shelves are filled with bric-à-brac. China dogs glare at you, lustre ware glistens, and mirrors at either side reflect again and again. Between the caravans children and lurchers sprawl and sleep under tarpaulins spread over iron hoops. Horse dealing, tin-smithing, palmistry, mushroom picking—the owners of these abodes will turn their hand to anything that brings in profit.

By two o'clock in the afternoon of that first day of the fair, the sides of the square in the town were lined with horse and donkey carts, and pigs and calves from the creels were changing hands. On the fairground, one street away, were tents and booths for all kinds of sports, merry-go-rounds, and swing boats. There was plenty of business, too; heavy cattle were being bought and sold, horses were being paced.

What was left of the square was filled with human beings and the lighter cattle. The hooting of any motor that tried to get through the throng was drowned by the bellowing of the beasts, the squealing of pigs, and the general turmoil of bargain-making. Accordions, fiddles, and street singers added variation to the major themes.

At the head of the square a three-tiered scaffolding, over fifty feet high, had been erected. Banners were being hoisted to its masts, strings of bunting were being draped about its balconies, electric lights fitted to its framework. By five o'clock in the afternoon the crowds had become so dense that it was difficult to move in the square. Wives and families of business men and other inhabitants of the town had emerged in their finery, gipsy mothers carrying their babies under bright shawls had crossed the river from their encampment, visitors were there in festive attire, and the clergy also had appeared, conspicuous in their black.

The procession was due to start at 5.30, but whether it was to be by God's time, which follows the sun—in Ireland twenty-five minutes later than in England—or by Old Time which follows Greenwich, or by New Time which corresponds to British Summer Time, nobody knew. As things turned out, it must have been by God's time, for it wasn't till seven o'clock British Summer Time that the head of the procession could be seen advancing up the hill. The parade was led by a dozen children on horseback, two abreast, the riders and their mounts decorated with sashes and trappings of green. Then came the Irish tricolour, and after it a kilted pipe band playing *The Minstrel Boy*. On the heels of the band marched boys dressed to represent the Fenians of 1798, and following them, on a large red motor lorry, King Puck himself, enthroned on a green pedestal under a golden canopy. Over his loins he wore a royal mantle of purple and white, and from tip to tip of his prodigious horns he carried a string of small brass bells. Four youths in ancient Irish dress stood beside him as bodyguard.

The parade marched through the square and, with band still playing, circled the town. Meanwhile children in green and white danced on the lower tier of the scaffold. Then, as the strains of the pipes were heard returning to the square, the dancing ceased and a table draped in green was moved into the centre of the stage. On the table was a golden crown. A young girl wearing a silver crown and the purple mantle of a queen took her place beside it.

Now a momentary hush fell on the assembly as the procession halted and the pipes ceased their chanting. In contrast to the young folk, hitherto most in evidence, strong men came forward and lifted Puck and his throne from the lorry to the stage awaiting him. Then with the national colours held high, with onlookers standing to attention, and the pipes playing *The Dawning of the Day*, the queen placed the golden crown on the goat's head. And now ropes and tackle were adjusted, and to the tune of *The Wearing of the Green* the king was hoisted to the topmost tier, there to remain and reign over the town for three days. During his rule no public-house closes day or night; there is dancing in the streets and houses of the town and in the tents on the fairground; every one is on holiday, though the main purpose of the fair, the buying and selling of cattle, is not forgotten. Then, on the evening of the 'scattering day,' Puck is brought down: his crown, his royal mantle, and his bells are taken from him, and he is set free among the hills to roam and exercise his natural rights for yet another year.

The inhabitants of Killorglin, while insisting that their annual festival is 'as old as time,' try nevertheless to find explanation for it in comparatively recent events, real or imagined: they do not like to feel that there is anything pagan in the ceremony. Yet, while granting that there isn't one heathen idea in their heads to-day, I think there can be no doubt that the origin of the fair is as pre-Christian as the bonfires on Midsummer's Eve, the worship at holy wells, or the giving of eggs, symbols of fertility, at Easter time.

Three days might seem long enough for such festivities, but in 1949 the celebrations became prolonged into a week. No sooner had 'the scattering' begun than it became known that Spanish Lad, a greyhound from Killorglin, had won the Irish Derby. Once again the band went into action, marching from the town to meet the dog and play it in. That night a bonfire blazed in the square and a table with barrels of porter stood in the open for every one to help himself 'with glass, cup, or bucket, whichever pleased him best.'

And then, as if that hadn't been enough gaiety for one week, a wedding among the gipsies was proclaimed for the following day. 'No hotel in Ireland would have more elegant tables,' I was told afterwards. 'You never saw the like of them, spread along the road among the caravans, with all the silver and the linen cloths and the jellies and the cutlery and the cakes and the hams—a power of money was spent on it all. And the drapers' shops was nearly sold out with all the clothes that were bought. The bride had on her a dress of blue, and every man was in his best, and the women with bright shawls, and handkerchiefs on their heads.'

There had been a little bit of trouble before the wedding because the bride and bridegroom were sort of cousins of each other, and the parish priest at Killorglin wouldn't marry them. The girl's mother said she'd have no tinker's wedding on the bridge, so they had to go into Killarney and get a dispensation from the bishop. Having surmounted that difficulty they were married in the church in Killarney, but they didn't waste any time after the ceremony before they hurried back to Killorglin. 'Let's get back to Puck and freedom,' was what they said: gipsies are not very popular with the authorities in Killarney. That evening four barrels of stout stood on the parapet of the bridge, three on one side for the men and one on the other for the women, 'for everything was very orderly.' And the bride's father sat outside his caravan inviting all the passers-by to come in for a whiskey or sherry or port, and there was the grandest singing and dancing all night. There hadn't been the like in Killorglin for years.

CHAPTER TWENTY-SEVEN

THERE ARE MOMENTS oft recurring in our lives when we long to be away from any sight of a house, from any sound of humanity; and yet if we do get away, within no time at all we are longing to hear a cough or even a snore from the next room.   Such were my feelings when late one evening, after a few days in the bogs, I pulled into the Caragh Lake Hotel which overlooks one of the loveliest stretches of water in Kerry.   Around the crescent margin of that lake, cloud-chequered hills pile up from east and west to south, culminating in the blue dome of Carrantuohill, 3,414 feet, the highest mountain in Ireland.

The lady in the room next to mine that night did not snore or even cough, for all I heard, but the following morning on the gravel outside the hotel she spoke to me.   One note of her voice and I knew her.   Forty years ago she had come to live within a few miles of my home. She was in mourning at the time for her parents who had died and left her a considerable property, and her grey eyes were sad and her ankles were trim and she rode a magnificent black horse, and whether it was for the horse or the property or the ankles or the sad eyes, I wanted to comfort her. I was prepared to lay myself and my palette at her feet. They were everything I had. And now, after all these years, we met again. She was in black as before, this time for the death of her husband, and her eyes held the same wistfulness and her ankles were as neat as ever and I wanted once again to say a word to comfort her. 'Go on with you,' she said, 'we're too near the Blarney stone,' and with that she stepped into her big black car, started off in second gear, and left me looking after her and thinking of the brown horse I used to ride that always seemed a stride behind her black.

However, that evening, as I was returning from making a drawing of one of the turf banks that stand like great platforms in the bogs, a girl arrived at the hotel from Dublin. She was on holiday from England where she taught science at a school in Dorset, and in a few days' time she was to meet her father in Waterville. He was an amateur antiquarian, she told me, and was following up the theory that the major stones in the megalithic circles were orientated to a particular feature in the landscape, such as a gap between hills or a peak behind which the sun rose at a turning-point of the year. There was one of these rings on a hill outside Waterville that he was anxious to see. I said it had been orientated to a very fine storm the day I was there. She asked me if I knew Dorset. I said only the downs and the swannery at Abbotsbury. She too had seen that amazing and unique colony of several hundred birds, with nest built up beside nest so that one can scarcely step between them. She too had wandered on the

chalk hills behind Lulworth and had seen the 'pillar stone,'
relic of a universal if outmoded faith, on Batcombe Down.
Did I know Dublin? she asked.   Well, yes, I said, I'd failed
several examinations there and I'd seen the corpses in St.
Michan's.   Then we discussed the vaults of that church and
the human remains, centuries old, which for some unex-
plained reason are as well preserved as the mummified relics
of the kings and queens of Egypt.   The coffins, like the
vaults, are open.   The bodies, with flesh and skin, can be
seen and touched.   Even their joints are loose: when one lifts
a hand, there is perfect freedom of movement at the wrist and
elbow.   The air is sweet and clean, there is not a trace of the
cadaverous about it.   It is interesting that there should be
such a profusion of spiders in those vaults, for in the tenth
century the site of the church was a vast oak forest, and
writing in 1571 Dr. Hamner, in his *Chronicle of Ireland*,
states: 'Anno 1095.   The faire green or Commune . . . was
all wood, and hee that diggeth at this day to any depth, shall
finde the ground full of great rootes.   From thence, *Anno*

1098, King *William Rufus*, by licence of *Murchard* (King of Leinster), had that frame which made up the roofe of Westminster Hall, where no English Spider webbeth or breedeth to this day.'

We didn't, of course, discuss all those details then. Other more interesting subjects occurred to us as the evening went on. We watched the shadows on the mountains grow fainter and fainter, hill merging into hill until the whole range became a stencilled backcloth. As the last vestiges of colour drained into the west, the lake was transformed into molten silver held in the ebony bowl of the hills. She mentioned that her name was Anne.

That night, thinking again of Dorset, I remembered a walk over the downs with Llewelyn Powys. As we came near to the grave of Caractacus he had grown solemn.

'We are both past middle age,' he said. 'Have you ever thought what final message you would like to leave as a result of your life's experience?'

'I 'd like to make a damn good joke and die smiling,' I said.

Llewelyn was shocked by this. 'No, no!' he said earnestly. 'You must be serious.'

'I am serious,' I told him. 'Few men are coherent at the end. Let them give vent to their wisdom in the heyday of their vitality, while their minds are still unclouded, but when they grow old let them smile at the futility of their own conceits.'

For myself, I may say that the only time I was near to being eligible for last words, I was quite incapable of uttering them, for I had just had a bullet through my neck. It had gone between the windpipe and the gullet and had left me in no fit state for public speaking. Nor, indeed, had I any wish at that particular moment to make an oration. My only feeling as I lay on that Gallipoli cliff was one of loneliness;

I felt that it wouldn't have mattered if only they had known at home. Gradually my legs became numb from the feet upwards, and I knew from experience of an anaesthetic that when sensation left the hips there would be no more. 'This is the end,' I thought. Then from far away I heard my name called. 'I've gone,' I thought. Again I heard the call, this time a little louder. It seemed funny that they should know my name; of all things I hadn't expected that. And then someone shook me roughly by the shoulder and bellowed into my ear. I opened my eyes, to see our regimental doctor bending over me. 'Come on,' he said, 'we must get you out of this.' And they did.

But such memories were not for long. My thoughts soon turned to Llewelyn's philosophy, 'the glory of life.' He once wrote to me: 'We should live every day as if we had been suddenly let out of our graves where for two centuries our diet had been dust and darkness.' Because of his tenuous grasp of life he was ever conscious of the annihilation of death. Every moment of life granted to him was a gold coin dropped into the purse of his experience. He too believed that regrets come to us more often from the rejection of opportunities than from the full savouring of their possibilities.

Next morning when I awoke at dawn the smoke-blue peak of Carrantuohill rose through a girdle of cloud. The lake was calm, and the reflection of the mountain sank as a mighty keel deep into the water. As the light strengthened a momentary breeze sent a shiver across the surface of the lake —heliotrope, rose, and silver, like the markings on a fish's side.

Later in the day Anne accepted an invitation to come with me for a drive. She had a book of Elizabethan poetry with her, which she would read if I found anything to draw.

Wheatears played hide-and-seek with us along the mountain roads, one moment perched on a wall dipping their tails as if in salute, at the next darting behind the stones or rocks, only to reappear a few yards ahead. We stopped the car beside a steel-blue shimmering lake. Coots were there in plenty, and sand-martins flying low over the water. On a narrow strip of waste land siskins were feeding on thistle heads, hanging upside down like tits, the bright yellow of their breasts a rich contrast to the purple petals above them. We left the car beside the road and followed the rocky course of a small river into the hills. Almost from under our feet a mallard rose, but, being in eclipse, it could only flap a few dozen yards before dropping into another pocket of bog.

The sun was hot. Bees were busy in the heather. We picked our way through patches of gorse; we sank knee-deep in bog; we clambered over rocks, crossing and recrossing the stream until we found ourselves beside a pool, deep and shadowed by an overhanging rock. Above where we stood the course of the stream was slashed with diagonal rocks over which the water tumbled and foamed. In the quiet pool before us, flecks of the foam followed the gentle eddies of the current. We sat down and watched them trace their arabesques of pattern.

'Why not make a drawing?' Anne suggested.

'Why not slip in and give me a subject?' I said.

'I was going to read.'

'I'll recite to you instead.'

'What will you recite?' she asked.

'How about this?' I said.

> '"My love in her attire doth show her wit,
>   It doth so well become her;

SWEET CORK OF THEE

For every season she hath dressings fit,
   For Winter, Spring, and Summer.
No beauty she doth miss
   When all her robes are on:
But Beauty's self she is
   When all her robes are gone.'''

CHAPTER TWENTY-EIGHT

To MY KNOWLEDGE I had never been in the town of Schull until I went there on 15th August to watch the regatta. I had left the van in a side street and was finding my way to the harbour when an old man accosted me.

'How are ye going on? Well, I hope?' Before I had time to reply, he added: ''Tis some years since you were in the town.'

'I was never here before,' I said.

'Oh then, you were,' he replied.

'Oh then, I wasn't,' I said.

He looked at me for a moment, tapped my chest with one finger and the stump of a second, and said very seriously: 'Didn't you pass through in Cotter's bread-van one night and you on your way to Goleen? 'Twould be about five or six years ago.'

'I did go to Goleen,' I said, 'and by bread-van, but it was dark and I couldn't see where I was.'

'You came through here and I was beside you from Bantry. The two of us was hunched up together alongside of the driver, and as we was passing the lakes you says to me: "Isn't the swans very white on the black water?" And I says to you: "Isn't the water very black agin the white swans?" And then says you: "The night is as black as the water," and I says to you: "There'll be a mist in the morning will be as white as the swans." And Mickey Ryan, from Clear Island, was behind in the bread with us. He'd gone on the booze and missed his ship, and when he went to find her she wasn't there. Blown up she was with a couple of

torpedoes.   Isn't it wonderful the way the Almighty looks
after some people?'

I asked if he could direct me to the harbour.   'Come with
me,' he said, 'and I'll put you on the straight road.'

We walked along the main street together, my guide having
a greeting for every one we met or passed.

'And did you have a good time at Goleen?' he continued.
'You did to be sure.   Wasn't it sad about poor McCormick
at the hotel?   Ah well, he had his day got, God rest his soul.
Isn't it wonderful weather?   Schull always has a fine day
for the regatta.   There was Bank Holiday at Kinsale and it
pouring, and at Baltimore 'twas no better.'

At this moment the intention of an old woman, with one of
the West Cork cloaks over her head, to cross a narrow lane
in front of us coincided with the intention of a motor lorry to
emerge from that lane.   I was only just in time to grip her
by the arm and pull her almost from under the wheels.

'Merciful heavens!' she exclaimed, looking up at me.
'Wouldn't eighty-eight be young to die?' She began to
shake all over with fright.

'Give me a hold of your arm, Mrs. Duggan,' said my companion, 'and I 'll see you home.' The two of them crossed the road and went westwards through the town, while as directed I turned down a winding hill towards the sea.

The regatta was already in full swing when I came in sight of the harbour, a pleasant circular expanse of water surrounded by low hills whose woods and fields slope gently to a rocky foreshore. There did not seem to be a great many boats taking part, but a big crowd of spectators had assembled, some of them sitting on the shingle above high-water mark, others on the grassy bank above the low cliffs. On the short pier, where normally nets and other fishing gear are spread and where men may be seen splicing ropes, trimming spars, or adjusting floats, vendors of ice-cream, soft drinks, and currant buns were driving their trade.

The committee boat was anchored a short distance from the pier head, and its loudspeaker was in full blast.

'Hallo there! Hallo there!' it called. 'There 's only two boats competing in the Sailing Dinghy race: Captain Cullinane's *Wee Win* and Mr. Patrick Murphy's *Lady Melba*. Captain Cullinane is a seventy-year-old sailor and has sailed the seven seas, and Mr. Patrick Murphy is a well-known pleasure-boat sailor. We expect to have a very close finish in this race. Pay attention now, Captain Cullinane and Paddy Murphy: the five-minute gun is going to be fired immediately.'

After a pause the speaker continued.

'Could we have a little music from the band now, please? Something lively we 'd like.' To this there was no response. The loudspeaker addressed us again. 'Hallo there! Will Mr. Patrick Mahony who is in charge of the band ask them to play up. Where are ye, Paddy? If ye 're above in the town, will ye get the boys together and give us some music?'

Again there was a pause until, in default of the band, the

loudspeaker itself blared out the words of *The Boys from County Cork*. How they licked the Black and Tans was interrupted by the news that the competing dinghies were coming up to the line.

'The two of them is coming in nicely to the start. Ten seconds to go. Keep her sailing, captain. O.K., Paddy, haul your sheet, we 're about to fire the shot!'

The two boats crossed the line within a second of each other. Soon came the next announcement:

'Those taking part in the First Class Pleasure Boat race will have to wait about half an hour because Colonel Chavasse when putting out his boat this morning stove in a plank and he 's having it fixed. We 're very sorry to delay, but we can't help. Would you kindly hurry up with the repairs, Colonel, because all the rest of the boats is waiting for you now.'

Then we were told of the 'All in' race for fishing yawls: first prize £5, second prize £2. 'This is a very novel race, never seen here before. Four boats taking part, sail and oar and engine and anything they 've got. If ye look east the harbour, I think Mr. O'Sullivan is having trouble with his peak halyard, but never mind, he has a good engine and he 'll get going yet. We 're calling on the *St. Mary* to know if she 's going to compete. That 'll make five. Give us a lift of your hat, *St. Mary*, if you 're joining in. Could we have a little music now, please? Would the band kindly play us a tune? Where are ye at all, Paddy?'

Presently the gun was fired, and as the yawls coursed away to the south the sun turned their tanned canvas to scarlet. The sails of the yachts, manœuvring about the harbour, shone white as the breasts of gulls.

What was to have been the big event of the day was next announced.

'We have grand weather to-day, thank God, but 'tis been very bad these past two weeks and that 's why we 're so short of yachts to-day. We have only the two of them: Mr. Patrick O'Keefe's *John Dory* and Father McCarthy's *Baroness*. As you remember, the *John Dory* won last year from eleven others. We had four boats from England last year and 'twas the best race we 've had for the hell of a long time. But the *Baroness* has a good handicap, and I 'm thinking it will be a close finish.'

This prophecy turned out to be true, for the *Baroness* won on time by three-quarters of a minute, only a little less close than the six seconds that divided the two sailing dinghies after a five-mile course.

And so the events continued. There were four-oar rowing races and two-oar rowing races and swimming races. It was late in the evening when the final event, the 'Pig and Pole,' took place. To-day there is no more than a flag at the end of the greasy pole, and the man who gets the flag doesn't even win a pig—the prize is a cash one. But on such occasions when I was a boy there was always a pig in a hamper swinging on the end of the pole, and the man who brought the animal ashore won it. Many the lively aquatic gymnastics I saw, for not only had the hamper to be opened but the pig carried to land through the water, and a pig rarely conforms to the precedents of life-saving.

One event that I remember at a regatta occurred at Bere-haven, not many miles from Schull, in 1917. That town is situated on the north coast of Bantry Bay and opposite to it, guarding the mouth of the bay, is Bere Island, at that time garrisoned by British troops. I was one of those stationed there. The regatta committee had invited our regimental band to perform for them and, permission being obtained, the event was held 'Under the Patronage of the Colonel and Officers of the 4th Battalion, Royal Munster Fusiliers.'

All went well. In the early afternoon the government launch made several trips to the mainland with troops on leave for the occasion, and in the evening it ferried most of them back again. Orders were that on the last journey of the day it was to take the officers and the band. In due course the colonel and the rest of us went aboard. But there was no sign of the band. The tide had gone down, and from the launch, low under the pier, we could see little of what was happening on the quay. We were chiefly conscious of the sergeant-major standing at the head of the gangway, waiting to deal with the musicians if and when they should appear. It was, of course, only fair and right that they should be entertained after giving their services to the community, but there was a danger that it might be overdone.

At last, one by one they came in sight, walking somewhat delicately along the quay. As each one reached the gangway, the sergeant-major took him by the shoulders and added just the impetus necessary to send him sliding down the smooth plank into the hold, his cornet, his trombone, or his drum clasped to his bosom.

The launch moved towards the island, the officers standing

on the bridge, the band lying in the hold, and soon we were mooring under the Union Jack that flew above headquarters. To the musicians this seemed the time for *God Save the King* which, in view of current political feeling, had not been played on the mainland. Now the programme could be completed in accordance with military tradition. Unfortunately, not one of them could get to his feet. But that did not inhibit their zeal. Heroes all, they played the anthem as they had fallen, not once but several times, including many unrehearsed variations, while the colonel and officers stood on the bridge at the salute.

CHAPTER TWENTY-NINE

LOOKING SOUTH FROM the pier at Schull one sees Cape Clear Island, the most southerly point of Ireland. There it was that St. Kieran was born and there, too, his first miracle was vouchsafed. It is told that one day while yet a boy he saw a hawk carry off a small bird that had been brooding its nestlings. The young Kieran, moved with a great pity, prayed earnestly 'and straightway the ravisher came down with his prey and laid the small bird, mangled and half dead, before him. But under the pitying gaze of the lad, the hapless creature by God's grace was made whole, to his heart's delight: and before his eyes sat brooding on her nest, happy and unhurt.' Many years later when, although by then a bishop, he was living as a hermit in 'a vast solitude, thick with forest,' animals came to him, 'a fox and a badger and a wolf and a deer: and they stayed with him, tame and gentle. And they obeyed the saint's word in all things, as if they had been his monks.' But one day the fox fell into sin, stealing his abbot's shoes and taking them to his former lair. 'Knowing this, the good Father sent another monk or disciple, namely the Badger, into the forest after the Fox, to bring back his brother to his post. So the Badger, being well learned in the woods, at once set out in obedience to his abbot's bidding, and took his way straight to the den of Brother Fox. There, finding him about to gnaw his master's slippers, he bit his ears and his tail, and cropped his fur, and forced him to come back with him to his monastery, there to do penance for his theft.' Thereafter the fox lived sociably with the others.

These words that I have quoted are from *Beasts and Saints*, translated from medieval narratives by Helen Waddell. Of all the books for which I have committed engravings, none has given me greater delight than this collection of stories. If at times they are a little difficult to take literally, they may at least be thought of as Pausanias regarded the legends of Greece. 'When I commenced to write my history,' he says, 'I had an inclination to regard these as foolishness, but on reaching Arcadia I began to hold a different view of them. In the days of old those Greeks who were thought to be wise spoke not straight out but in parables and so I considered these legends to be one form of Greek wisdom.' Many a true word is spoken in myth. There is scarcely a legend that isn't a parable.

In fable the badger has always played the part of a gentle, peace-loving creature, a cousin of the fox whom he tries in vain to lead into the way of virtue. In fact the badger is gentle and inoffensive unless attacked. It is sociable by nature, often paying calls on its neighbours. Its setts are scrupulously tidy, its habits cleanly. Most of the crimes of which it has been accused may more properly be attributed to the fox.

Clear Island, or Cape Clear as it is more generally known, is wild and wind-blown, bare of all trees. At the head of Trakieran, 'the Strand of Kieran,' is a pillar stone with crosses incised upon it, front and back, which it is believed was put there by the saint with his own hands before he set out on his missionary labours, even before the coming of St. Patrick. Towards the northern end of the island there is another standing stone, a relic perhaps of an earlier faith. It has a hole through it, and I was told that 'you couldn't marry a girl unless you could kiss her through that hole, but sure you 'd want the face of a duck to manage it.'

'Holed stones' are numerous in Ireland and occur also in

England, Scotland, France, India, and other parts of the world. With most of them there is a tradition either of healing powers or of the ratification of compacts. Where the hole is large enough, the postulant crawls through, leaving behind him his sins or his affliction. Ailing children are passed through as a remedy for their weakness. Where the holes are smaller, clothes and cloths are treated in a similar manner, that they may relieve suffering; or hands are clasped from either side at the exchange of marriage vows. The symbolism of a wedding ring may well have a direct connection with that of these stones.

Clear Island is about three miles in greatest length, and there are between two and three hundred people living there to-day. 'There are some very wealthy men on the island,' said the skipper of the launch in which I crossed from the mainland. 'One of them has eight cows and another as many as five or maybe six.' Farming and fishing are the two main sources of livelihood. There are times when 'the fish in the south harbour are that thick that if you fell into the sea you'd float on them.'

At the western extremity of the island, some two hundred feet above the sea, is a lake so alkaline in its properties that 'if you put the roughest old bit of a rag in it, covered in tar and paint, and left it there for a week or a fortnight, 'twould come out like a handkerchief.' So I was told by a woman who was spreading dirty clothes in the water with stones on their corners to anchor them. From further along the shore I could see four buckets, filled with clothes, submerged in the water. There are no fish in the lake, but there are two species of fresh-water shrimp in plenty. '"Camoges," we call them,' said Johnny Burke of the Shamrock House where I was staying. ''Tis them that does the most of the cleaning. Sure, you 'd feel them nibbling at your feet when you go into the water. There was a professor or something from Oxford came here and, says he, they 're kind of descended from lobsters. Great God Almighty, when he showed me one under the magnification instrument he had with him, 'twas like a three-foot crayfish!'

Communications with the mainland are by mail boat to Baltimore, a small fishing village that gave its name to a settlement in America which in little more than three hundred years has grown to be a city of nearly a million inhabitants. There is no record of the founding of Baltimore in Ireland; its name in Irish, *Baile-an-tighe-mhoir*, means 'the town of the large house,' no doubt derived from the ancient castle of the O'Driscolls whose ruins are still conspicuous in the landscape. We have, however, some details of the earliest days of its namesake city on the other side of the Atlantic. The name was conferred upon it by George Calvert, Lord Baltimore, who derived his title from the town in Ireland, and who in 1632 had obtained a grant of territory in Maryland from King Charles I.

'Captaine Iohn Smith, sometimes Governour of the

Country,' telling of the Indians who till then had been its sole inhabitants, writes: 'Some are of disposition feareful, some bold, most cautelous, all savage, soone moved to anger, and so malicious that they seldome forget an injury. For their apparell they are sometimes covered with the skinnes of wilde beasts, but the common sort have scarce to cover their nakednesse, but with grasse, the leaves of trees, or such like.' Some of the women 'have their legs, hands, breasts, and face cunningly imbrodered with divers markes, as beasts, serpents, artificially wrought into their flesh with black spots.' Of the men he says that one carried in a hole pierced in the ear 'a small greene and yellow coloured snake, neare halfe a yard in length, which crawling and lapping her selfe about his necke oftentimes familiarly would kisse his lips.' Others of the men preferred a dead rat as ornament, others 'the hand of an enemy dryed.' Their heads and shoulders were painted red with 'many formes of paintings . . . he is the most gallant that is the most monstrous to behold.'

Captain Smith finishes his account by referring to the future city: 'So then here is a place, a nurse for souldiers, a practise for mariners, a trade for marchants, a reward for the good, and that which is most of all, a businesse (most acceptable to God) to bring such poore Infidels to the knowledge of God and his holy Gospell.' Two hundred years later the town was recognized as the centre of the domestic slave trade, the poor infidels of slaves being brought across the Atlantic from Africa in fast Baltimore clippers.

In the year 1631 (when the first settlers there were taking up land, among them one David Jones who 'patented three hundred and eighty acres at a rent of fifteen shillings two and one-half pence per annum' and gave his name to the river around whose lower reaches the city has since grown) a terrible disaster befell the town of Baltimore in County Cork.

On the night of 20th June, two Barbary corsairs sailed into the harbour, landed their men and having plundered the place carried off a large number of its inhabitants to be sold in the slave markets of Algiers. Father Pierre Dan, a French missionary then working in Algeria, states that the total of those taken numbered two hundred and thirty-seven men, women, and children. He writes: 'It was a pitiable thing to see them exposed for sale, wives separated from their husbands, children from their fathers. They sell the husband on one side and the wife on the other, tearing away the daughter from her mother's arms so that there is no hope of them ever seeing each other again.' He describes the detailed scrutiny by prospective buyers, when the naked captives were made to walk, jump, and caper; the examination of their teeth and eyes, and the careful study of their appearance in order to deduce whether their disposition was good or bad. 'But above all things they look most closely at the hands; and for two reasons. First, to judge by the delicacy or hardness if they are manual workers; and the second, which is the chief, so that by Chirognomy, to which they are much addicted, though the study is vain and ridiculous, they should be able to discover by the lines and signs which they see there, if such slaves will live long, if they have any sign of illness, of danger, of mischance; or even if in their hands their escape is marked. Now, those who are accustomed to practise these precautions, do it so that by this knowledge they may know whether or not to risk their money in the purchase of the Unfortunates, so much has avarice the empire over the hearts of such tyrants.'

From the beginning of the seventeenth century, when the pirates of the Barbary coast had acquired the art of ship-building and had substituted vessels carrying sail for the galleys propelled by oars, their depredations spread further and further from their own coasts. Hitherto they had confined their activities to the western Mediterranean; now they were able to go as far west as Madeira, taking from there in 1617 as many as twelve hundred prisoners. Ten years later many hundreds were taken from Denmark and Iceland. In 1634 Father Pierre estimated that there were twenty-five thousand Christian slaves in the city and neighbourhood of Algiers, and he reckoned that the Algerian pirates had not less than seventy sailing cruisers, all of them 35–40-gun ships. On 7th August of that year, he saw 'twenty-eight of the best of them sail in quest of Norman and English ships which usually came to Spain at that season to take in wine, oil, and spices.' Altogether, the combined fleets of Tunis, Algiers, and Morocco numbered one hundred and twenty sailing ships besides twenty-five galleys and other vessels. For three centuries, from the time of Barbarossa until after the Congress of Aix-la-Chapelle in 1818, a voyage in the Mediterranean was a perilous adventure. Early in the seventeenth century, four hundred British ships were seized by the pirates within four years.

No distinctions of class were made among the captured except towards those of high rank who, for encouragement in seeking their ransom, were often treated with greater harshness than the others. Of all who suffered enslavement by these pirates none can have been more distinguished than Don Miguel de Cervantes who, when returning from Naples, was captured and held as a slave for five years. It is told of him in captivity that when after threats of torture and death he still refused to compromise a friend, the Dey, far from carrying out his threats, purchased the poet from his owner at a high price.

In 1659 the Earl of Inchiquin, 'Murrough of the Burnings,' was among those taken; he spent seven months in captivity before he was released for a ransom of 7,500 crowns. It isn't likely that much sympathy went to him from Ireland. One wonders if the flames of Adare Abbey and of the Rock of Cashel with its thousands of victims ever came to his mind during his incarceration.

Baltimore is not the only name on the map of America that has a direct connection with the south coast of Ireland, for it was in Cork that William Penn, the founder of Pennsylvania, first came in contact with the religious ideals which eventually brought about the creation of that state. His father, Admiral Penn, had been rewarded by Cromwell for his victory over the Dutch fleet by the gift of Macroom Castle, and it was while the son was living there that he met Thomas Loe, then preaching Quakerism in Cork. Loe came from Oxford, and when William, under the patronage of Charles II, went to Oxford University he met Loe again. From then on it was for him a fight not only for a religious principle but for freedom of thought. He was expelled from his college because it was said that his puritan way of life led to quarrels and fighting. A Presbyterian minister denounced him for blasphemy, after which he spent nine months in the Tower. In London he was arrested as a rioter and imprisoned for preaching in the street.

But because of the king's promise to his friend the admiral to look after his son, William was received at court, and though at first his manner there created some amusement he soon came to be respected by Charles and his courtiers. There is a story that one day, when in the presence of the king, Penn neglected as a matter of principle to remove his hat. Thereupon the king took off his own.

'Friend Charles,' said Penn, 'why hast thou removed thy hat?'

'Friend William,' replied the king, 'it is because it is the custom of this place that only one should remain covered.'

Q

Gradually the picture formed in Penn's mind of a state where everybody should be free and equal and all should worship as they thought fit. To the west of the Delaware River there lay a tract of land nearly as large as England. Penn obtained a grant of this from the king, in payment of a debt of £16,000 owing to his father. When in March 1680 he was summoned to Whitehall to receive the charter, the only point remaining to be settled was a name for the new colony. Penn wished to call it New Wales, because of the mountainous character of the land, but a Welshman objected.

'Sylvania,' suggested Penn as an alternative, the land being also rich in forests.

'Pennsylvania,' said the king.

It was a Friday when I left Baltimore to return to Gougane. During August and September Friday in Bantry is fair day for sheep, cattle, horses, and young pigs. On Thursdays the speciality is fat pigs. I arrived in the town during the early afternoon and the first man I met as I stepped out of the van was Teigue the Pass. He hadn't come to buy sheep or to sell them—he just wanted to see the way prices were going.

A short, thickset man had a flock of mixed sheep—ewes, wethers, lambs, and rams—herded into a corner, watched over by a boy in a green jersey, a man in a red one, and a golden collie. A double deal was in progress, for while a butcher was bargaining for the rams, a farmer was after the lambs, eight of them.

The butcher was pinching the rams close to the tail—''tis the leg of mutton he's thinking of,' said Teigue. The farmer was prodding the lambs about the loins—''tis bone for breeding he is after,' said Teigue.

'Three pounds a head,' said the butcher.

'Four pound ten,' said the owner.

'Four pounds ten! When has rubber gone to that? God Almighty, you 'd put one bite of them in your mouth of a Saturday and you 'd have lockjaw by the Monday.'

The would-be purchaser of the lambs came forward. 'How much for the eight?' he asked.

'Two twelve six a head,' said the owner.

The buyer walked off as if in disgust, but he hadn't gone far before he turned and came back. 'Twenty pounds for the eight,' he said.

'Two twelve six,' said the owner.

'Ah, make a sale, man—make a sale, man,' called a voice from the crowd.

'They 're sold already,' said the owner.

'Sold?'

'Yes—to the man that gives the price.'

'And wouldn't you meet him?'

'I 'll meet him with the value for his money.'

As Teigue crossed the road to look at some young pigs a man stepped up to me. His face and his head had as little hair on them as his leggings or his boots, and all four of them were as red as each other. 'I have a horse would suit you,' he said.

'I don't want a horse,' I said.

'Listen a while,' he said. 'The horse that I 've got is more of an armchair than an animal.'

'I don't want an armchair,' I said.

'He 's so easy over a fence you 'd fall asleep on his back.'

Teigue rescued me before I fell asleep.

I had no wish to acquire cattle, sheep, piglets, or armchairs, so after watching a few more bargains being struck I made my way to the van, and having circumvented the traffic in the town drove quietly homewards.

Near Ballylicky a heron was fishing in the tidal water. It struck at a fish, caught it, held it a moment before swallowing, then flapped its wings and shook itself, before settling again to watch. Swallows were flying high in the valley of the Ouvane, glinting blue in the sunlight; a kestrel swooped across the road, showing the russet of its back. Against the evening light the ears of young rabbits shone red as the fuchsias in the hedges.

CHAPTER THIRTY

ALWAYS A WELCOME awaiting me at Gougane. Connie at the back door, just home from a day on the mountains with the sheep, or at the front door just going fishing on the lake, smiling. Nell in the hall or at the door of the dining-room, smiling; Eileen at the door of the dining-room or in the hall, smiling. Mary and Jer in the kitchen, smiling. Joan comes in from the bar with a glass in her hand for me. 'You must be tired now,' she says. Batty Kit comes in through the back door and sits down. Joan brings 'a drop' for him, too. 'Every good luck to you,' says Batty, clinking his glass against mine and shaking hands. A day or a week or a month or five years away, and when I get back everything is the same. I've never heard a cross word in that green Valley Desmond, I've never heard a child cry. In that womb among the hills there is the peace of the unborn. Time passes imperceptibly as the growth of a child.

My tale is told. Gougane is fifty miles to the west. Already the *Innisfallen* is berthed beside the quay, waiting to sail eastwards to Fishguard. Spacious and gracious the streets of Cork city, gracious and gentle the people. Nowhere is there a more double-handed welcome to one who offers but a finger of friendship; nowhere more time to show goodwill, nowhere more time for a passing word or joke.

There are places in this world where if you make an ambiguous remark you are sure to be misunderstood, but in Cork your kindliest meaning will be taken for granted. In

Cork, too, there is a natural grandeur of language. I ask a
bus conductor if there is room for me inside. 'There is
ample accommodation,' he replies. I inquire if someone
has been seen in the town and am told: 'I have no knowledge
of his travels.'

To walk in the city is as good as a tour through Europe.
You look down one side street and you see Dieppe, another
alongside of it and you are reminded of Oxford, another
and you think of Italy. And the city also possesses a splendour of its own. Where else, may I ask, of an evening but
by Patrick's Bridge will you see lavender-coloured mullet
weaving their courses among the reflected scarlet neon signs
of Denny's Bacon and Paddy Whiskey? Where else at noon-
day will you see a platoon of philosophers sitting on the rim
of a fountain, adding daily to the mirror-like polish of its
stones? In any other city the taps would be leaking. Where
else will you see policemen whose aesthetic activities would
be an inspiration to any choreographer? Exquisitely
drilled, a guarda on point duty in Cork city displays a more
varied repertoire of mime in half an hour than a London
policeman could demonstrate in twenty years. And, no
doubt influenced by this spirit of ballet, all pedestrians move
about the streets with as little regard for the traffic as Kerry
cattle on a mountain track.

> 'On these I ponder
> Where'er I wander,
> And thus grow fonder,
> Sweet Cork, of thee.'

In the Afghani language there is a saying: 'Every one thinks
his native country is a Kashmir.' Maybe they do. Ten
years ago I stated in print that Cork is the loveliest city in the
world, and no one has ever contradicted me. Now I declare

that Cork people are the loveliest in the world, and to them,
as I close, I give the old toast:

> 'Here's health and life to you,
> The man or woman of your choice to you.
> Land without rent to you,
> And death in Ireland.'

LOVELY IS THE LEE

Robert Gibbings

Lovely is the Lee, a beautifully illustrated book with wonderful wood engravings, begins in Galway, far away from the source of the Lee. A tour around Connemara gives us some pleasant sketches of púcáns, donkey-carts and cottages; Cong brings us antiquities, flint arrow heads and the like. Next we find ourselves in Inisbofin and in Aran and then we find ourselves in Cork – which Robert Gibbings claims is the loveliest city in the world:

> Cork is the loveliest city in the world. Anyone who doesn't agree with me either was not born in the city or is prejudiced. The streets are wide, the quays are clean, the bridges are noble ... It is such a friendly city, too. People that you never met in your life stop you in the street ...

THE FARM BY LOUGH GUR

Mary Carbery

The Farm by Lough Gur is the true story of a family who lived on a farm by Lough Gur, the Enchanted Lake, in County Limerick. Their home, shut away from the turmoil of politics, secure from apprehension of unemployment and want, was a world in itself.